THE ETHICAL EDUCATOR

PETER LANG
New York • Washington, D.C./Baltimore • Bern
Frankfurt am Main • Berlin • Brussels • Vienna • Oxford

THE ETHICAL EDUCATOR

Integrating Ethics within the Context
of Teaching and Teacher Research

Edited by Susan E. Israel
& Cynthia A. Lassonde

PETER LANG
New York • Washington, D.C./Baltimore • Bern
Frankfurt am Main • Berlin • Brussels • Vienna • Oxford

Library of Congress Cataloging-in-Publication Data

The ethical educator: integrating ethics within the context of teaching
and teacher research / edited by Susan E. Israel, Cynthia A. Lassonde.
p. cm.
Includes bibliographical references and index.
1. Teaching–Moral and ethical aspects. 2. Teachers–Professional ethics.
I. Israel, Susan E. II. Lassonde, Cynthia A.
LB1027.E77   371.102–dc22   2007010596
ISBN 978-1-4331-0160-1 (hardcover)
ISBN 978-1-4331-0159-5 (paperback)

Bibliographic information published by **Die Deutsche Bibliothek**.
Die Deutsche Bibliothek lists this publication in the "Deutsche
Nationalbibliografie"; detailed bibliographic data is available
on the Internet at http://dnb.ddb.de/.

Cover photograph by Susan E. Israel, taken at Trinity College, Dublin

The paper in this book meets the guidelines for permanence and durability
of the Committee on Production Guidelines for Book Longevity
of the Council of Library Resources.

© 2007 Peter Lang Publishing, Inc., New York
29 Broadway, 18th floor, New York, NY 10006
www.peterlang.com

Printed in the United States of America

Contents

Part II ∝ **Ethical Commitment to Teacher Research: The Classroom, the University, the Dilemma**

Foreword

Nearly three-quarters of a century have passed since Stuart Chase, the author of *The Tyranny of Words* (1938), wrote an essay titled "The Luxury of Integrity." He ranked the amount of freedom for integrity to be found within occupations and professions. He placed professors about midway on his scale.

I found that essay while I was searching for information on ethics in education years ago. As part of my search, I collected newspaper articles containing the word "ethics" in their headline. For a year I built my collection, and at the end of the year I had found news articles relating to ethics in law, medicine, journalism, athletics, business—but virtually none on education.

That search took place nearly thirty years ago, and I wrote about it in *Pitt*, a periodical published by the University of Pittsburgh (August 1979). In my essay, "Questions of Ethics," I raised a number of questions, many of which are still relevant today:

- Do we encourage an honest exchange of ideas between and among faculty, students, staff, and administrators?
- What do we do when we see image passing for substance? Educational fads? Misleading claims?
- Do we remain silent when we hear backbiting or character assassination?
- Do we restrain ourselves from speaking up for fear of reprisal?

There are more questions of course. We can all make our own lists.

The maxim that "speech is silver but silence is golden" may tell us how to get along or ahead in this world, but it says little about ethical behavior. The extent to which we are willing to speak up is a measure of the spirit of our freedom and our trust in humanity.

Many schools and colleges (as well as businesses and government agencies) have a person who serves as an ombudsman. We can go a step further: if as individuals, even with tenure, we find it difficult and dangerous to ask questions, a group can be set up within each educational institution with the charge and responsibility of asking questions. (For example: Why are we using these tests? If research shows that students score higher on state-mandated tests using computers, why do we require students to take those tests using pencils and paper? You can think of more questions to ask politely.) The loyal opposition in education would be similar to the loyal opposition that is an established part of many governments in the world.

The chapter writers in this collection have spoken up, raising questions and observations on a myriad of topics:

- teaching in Harlem and small towns
- role models and relationships with students
- coping with mandated testing, slogans, labels, and mislabels
- school–college partnerships, the ivory tower
- basic and applied research, advising
- the role of trust in teaching and research
- consuming research, writing clearly, listening silently and actively, advocating for students, children's stories, idealism, and reality
- dealing with students who have special needs, knowing the students' world, and many more topics

As stated so eloquently by my son, Jon Henry, whom I asked to review this foreword, it would be a sudden jump to say, "When you dip into this volume you will find a world of knowledge about ethics in education." Jon Henry realized that teachers can make stronger connections between why asking questions about ethics and making these observations reveals "ethics." If the root of ethics is never to stop observing or asking questions on that ever-lasting quest to find what is right, then when you dip into this volume you will find a world of knowledge about ethics in education.

Allen Berger

Preface

It is, therefore, essential that we continually reflect on our research to be sure that it is not only sound scientifically but that it makes a positive contribution to the educational enterprise.
—*American Educational Research Association, 2000, p. 1*

It is essential to educate teachers to engage in research to reflect on their practices and increase their instructional effectiveness, and to understand their responsibility to adhere to the highest of ethical standards. The editors of this book are passionate about teacher research, and so we joined the International Reading Association's Teacher Research Special Interest Group. As educators who have a combined interest in addressing, and desire to address, the need to help teacher researchers, we present here a comprehensive volume on teacher research that is a guide to the essential elements associated with teacher research.

After we put out a call for manuscripts to the Teacher Research Special Interest Group members and professional literacy organizations, such as the National Reading Conference, the interest to participate was immense. This book is derived from the *Comprehensive Guide to Teacher Research* (Lassonde & Israel, in press), published by the International Reading Association, the first book to focus exclusively on the ethics of teaching and teacher research in today's classrooms. Here, we establish through research and personal experiences why it is a teacher's moral duty to engage in research and teaching that is based on the highest ethical standards.

The Ethical Educator: Integrating Ethics within the Context of Teaching and Teacher Research is about the ethics of teaching and teacher research. As acknowledged in the epigraph to this preface, from the American Educational Research Association (AERA), the professional organization for teachers and researchers, educators are to reflect continually on their teaching practice and professional development goals relating to research. The premise for the two parts of this book is derived from the ethical standards of researchers. This book explains how to reflect on ethical standards and integrate them into the context of teacher research so that the research contributes to the profession.

The intended audience for this book includes all teachers who wish to reflect on their practices from an ethical and moral perspective, educators who are engaging in research within the classroom or outside of it, and those in higher education who support teacher researchers, as well as any educator or researcher who wants to understand ethical standards within the context of teaching and researching.

Reflections about Integrating Ethics within the Context of Teacher Research

Susan E. Israel

As a recipient of one of the teacher research grants funded by the International Reading Association, I am passionate about teacher research. The topic of the ethical standards of teachers and researchers is not usually discussed, but it seems to be somewhat implicit in education. As researchers, we are expected to know and understand how to apply ethical standards. Through my teaching experiences, I have realized that an ethical educator is something all teachers want to aspire to become. However, what I have discovered is that oftentimes ethical behavior seems to mirror a teacher's pedagogy. For example, is it ethical to label students in the early primary grades as high-achieving readers or struggling readers? When we conduct research in the classroom, should the results be shared openly with parents and other teachers if they reveal information that might hinder how future teachers come to know a student? Since I struggled with placing students in reading groups on the basis of ability, I struggle with the ethical decision to label readers at an early age. Therefore, my pedagogical beliefs would be similar to my ethical beliefs. But how can I use the highest ethical standards to guide my teaching and my research to enhance teaching and student learning?

Reflections about Integrating Ethics within the Context of Teacher Research

Cynthia A. Lassonde

When I think about being an ethical researcher, I think about how I would want to be treated as the participant or the reader of a research study—the age-old "Do unto others" golden rule philosophy. As a participant whose behaviors and comments will potentially be exposed and picked apart, I would want some consideration for how I was being presented to others. And I would want to be reassured that the researcher would check with me first to verify my meaning. As a student, I certainly would not want someone to display my work and personal files without the protection of anonymity if I chose it. As the parent of a student participant, I would want to be sure that my child did not feel coerced into being a part of a study because the researcher was her teacher. And, finally, as a reader, I would want to know that the researcher upheld the moral responsibilities of knowing right from wrong and practicing ethical fairness in the process. If I cannot trust the researcher was ethical, then I cannot believe the implications or results gleaned.

We are not born knowing right from wrong as children. Our family and community teach us and reinforce acceptable behaviors that build a moral foundation. Ethics is something a teacher researcher learns through direct instruction and develops over time. I learned a great deal about the ethics of research by talking with professors, by revising institutional review board research proposals, and by making my own mistakes. There was never any resource to pick up in which I could read about the ethics involved in teacher research, though. That is why I am excited about working on this project with Susan. This collection of essays on issues in teacher research ethics is the book I wish I had had when I was first trying to piece together the unknown rules of conduct of research. I think it will be an invaluable go-to tool not only for those just beginning to reflect on their classroom practices but also for veteran researchers looking to extend and sharpen their already developing integration of ethics in the context of teacher research.

How to Read This Book

The writing style used in this book is essay or retrospective personal narrative. Each author reflected retrospectively on his or her teaching experiences for the purpose of self-evaluation of experiences as an ethical educator. The purpose of writing in this style was to encourage the authors to add a personal dimension of teaching, philosophical beliefs, and ethical approaches relating to teaching, students, and the profession. Authors were invited to reflect on four areas:

- Reasons for becoming a teacher and an overview of their pathway to their current teaching position. Authors describe personal experiences or influential people that helped shaped who they are as an ethical educator today and their rationale focusing on a particular line of teacher research
- Specific strategies for handling difficult situations in an ethical manner in their teaching and research
- Challenges relating to teacher research that helped them bridge the gap between their philosophical approach and ethical decision making

- A synthesis of ethical lessons learned, in part, from their teaching, research, and retrospective reflections

As the volume editors, we are excited to offer a book that will help teachers think about ethical behaviors within the context of their research. We hope to make the case that being aware of ethical standards will decrease the number of unexpected issues associated with research that are not explained in teacher research guidelines. With that, we would like teacher researchers to use this book as a reflection tool to help guide or inform moral duties and decision making.

Susan E. Israel
Cynthia A. Lassonde

CR 1

INTRODUCTION
The Ethical Teaching Mind — Philosophical and Pedagogical Perspectives

Susan E. Israel

The members of the group are committed to values that are the foundation of a democratic society—freedom to teach, write, and study in an atmosphere conducive to the best interests of the profession.

—*Code of Ethics, International Reading Association (IRA)*

Chapter Overview

- Understanding the meaning of being an ethical educator.
- Reflecting on ethical standards of teaching and research.
- Discovering the author's personal insight into integrating ethical standards in teaching.

Inspirational Reflection

I am a member of the International Reading Association (IRA). I also adhere to IRA's Code of Ethics summarized in the epigraph at the opening of this chapter. The IRA is a group of literacy professionals committed to the development of a literate society.

To achieve the values of a democratic society, IRA members are guided by two standards. Members are held to ethical standards in professional relationships and ethical standards for reading professionals. In the best interest of my profession and love of literacy, I like to read books outside of my field so as to broaden my knowledge base and see how new information changes my own philosophical and pedagogical perspectives. As I reviewed the contents of one of my newest books by Ralph McInerny (2006), Professor of Philosophy and Director of the Jacques Maritain Center at Notre Dame, I realized that reflection plays a key role in ethical conduct. One needs to be aware of the code of ethics of one's profession and to reflect constantly on how the standards fit into teaching. Certain questions are raised in my mind: How does my conduct influence someone's opinion of me? To what degree does my ethical behavior influence my credibility? Does my personality or age play a role in my ethical decision making?

In *Merriam-Webster's Collegiate Dictionary*, 11th Edition, ethics is defined as the discipline dealing with what is good and bad and with moral duty and obligation. Ethics is also defined as a set of principles, a theory or system of moral values. To be ethical means to conform to accepted standards of conduct or behavior.

Codes of ethics are established to communicate principles that guide groups, professions, and organizations that abide by a set of agreed-upon standards. Three professional associations' codes of ethics that are important to conducting research relating to literacy are those of the National Education Association (NEA), the American Educational Research Association (AERA) and the International Research Association. The NEA, in the preamble to its code of ethics, formulates the following acceptable behaviors of the educator:

> The educator; believing in the worth and dignity of each human being, recognizes the supreme importance of the pursuit of truth, devotion to excellence, and the nurture of the democratic principles. Essential to these goals is the protection of freedom to learn and to teach and the guarantee of equal educational opportunity for all. The educator accepts the responsibility to adhere to the highest ethical standards. (1975, p. 1)

According to the NEA, an ethical educator is guided by two main principles: a commitment to the student and a commitment to the profession. The commitment to the student means that an educator shall not

- restrain a student from the pursuit of knowledge
- deny a point of view
- suppress or distort subject matter
- expose a student to harmful conditions
- allow factors such as race or religion to get in the way of student learning
- engage in professional relationships with students for personal gain
- disclose information about students obtained in the course of professional service unless disclosure serves a compelling professional purpose or is required by law

The commitment to the profession, according to NEA guidelines, means that an educator shall not

- make false statements or misrepresent professional qualifications
- assist entry to the profession of a person known to be unqualified or make false statements about that person
- assist a noneducator in the practice of teaching
- make false statements or disparage a colleague
- accept gratuities that might impair or influence professional decisions or actions

The AERA's code of ethics' standards state that educators have a responsibility to respect research populations, have intellectual ownership, and insist that research reviews meet high standards, maintain ethical integrity of research and ensure competence of novice students. Each of the six standards identifies specific guidelines. Researchers, regardless of discipline, adhere to these ethical expectations. The ethical standards set forth by the AERA in 2000 remind researchers that "[i]t is, therefore, essential that we continually reflect on our research to be sure that it is not only sound scientifically but that it makes a positive contribution to the educational enterprise" (p. 1).

Ethical Lessons to Be Learned

In summary, the ethical standards set forth by the NEA, the AERA, and the IRA clearly communicate the significance of the moral duty and obligations of those conducting research within the discipline of teacher education and literacy. Researchers have a responsibility to conform to accepted standards of moral conduct and ethical behavior set forth by their profession. Without a code of ethics, research and researchers would be open to criticism for not making positive contributions to education.

Part I of this book discusses ethical standards relating to teaching dilemmas. The contributors guide the reader on a reflective journey that allows for a more explicit view of what it means to be an ethical educator. The following questions are raised:

Chapter 2: How does pedagogy reflect ethical decision making?
Chapter 3: Does ethnicity factor into teaching and curriculum decision making?
Chapter 4: Do teacher screening procedures play a role in ethics?
Chapter 5: Does confidentiality constrain teachers?
Chapter 6: Should teachers pay more attention to the ethical actions of

their peers?

Chapter 7: Should researchers be concerned about institutional review boards?

Part II shifts to the act of conducting teacher research and specific issues that accompany teacher research in the classroom and in the greater school community. The contributors offer valuable insights based on personal experiences that invite the reader to consider the ethical aspects associated with research and learning. These ethical insights are brought to the forefront through the contributors' answers to the following questions:

Chapter 8: How do community and culture influence ethical teaching?

Chapter 9: How can teachers design research guided by the ethical requirements of teaching students with special needs?

Chapter 10: Are teachers guided by research inspired by affective domains of student learning?

Chapter 11: Is silence reflective of the inability to communicate thoughts based on fears imposed by others?

Chapter 12: What does it mean to be an ethical educator in the classroom?

Chapter 13: Is it important to consider students' perspectives when doing research?

Chapter 14: Who is responsible for one's research agenda?

Chapter 15: What is the role of ethics in collaborative research?

Chapter 16: What can we learn from the stories the contributors in this volume share?

Questions for Consideration

As a teacher or researcher, identify the ethical standards of your professional organization and reflect on your own practice and the ethical decisions you make. Do you feel limited in making ethical teaching decisions because of policies or beliefs?

Reflect on any ethical issues you are currently struggling with or have recently overcome in your teaching experiences. Can you adjust your teaching behaviors in response to the struggles you have faced when applying ethical ways of thinking?

Supplementary Resources

Overcoming Teacher Challenges: Watske, J., Daunt, P., & Moreno, R. (2002). Field supervision of ACE teachers. In M. Pressley (Ed.), *Teaching service and alternative teacher education.* Notre Dame, IN: University of Notre Dame Press. This professional development resource chapter gives firsthand accounts of the challenges first-year teachers face, specifically in relation to teacher service programs in underresourced and diverse communities. Teachers provide advice on how to overcome challenges relating to all aspects of teaching. Educators will benefit from this book because of the emphasis on dealing with difficult situations in diverse classrooms.

Exemplary Professors' Ethical Teaching Strategies: Bain, K. (2004). *What the best college teachers do.* Cambridge, MA: Harvard University Press. It is the responsibility of the university and professor in teacher education programs to guide future teachers to adhere to the highest of ethical standards. This book explains how some of the best college professors integrate ethics into all aspects of teaching, research, and service. Teachers will benefit from this book because the author does an excellent job of gathering stories from exemplary professors across disciplines and from diverse backgrounds.

Integrating Ethics in the Classroom: Mandela, R. N. (2002). *Nelson Mandela's favorite African folktales.* New York: W.W. Norton & Company. This book uses children's literature to help students learn about making ethical decisions. Nelson Mandela collected oral folktales that have been told in Africa for many years. The stories use mystical portrayals of animals and humans to communicate ethical lessons about living in the community and dealing with life's challenges. Teachers at all grade levels can read the short stories as conversation starters on ethical topics.

References

American Educational Research Association (2000). *Ethical Standards.* Retrieved December 9, 2006, from http://www.aera.org.

McInerny, R. (2006). *I alone have escaped to tell you: My love and pastimes.* Notre Dame, IN: University of Notre Dame Press.

National Education Association (1975). *Code of Ethics of the Education Profession.* Retrieved July 6, 2006, from http://www.nea.org/aboutnea/code.

Part I

ETHICAL COMMITMENT TO TEACHING

The Profession,
the Standards,
the Dilemmas

ᏯᎡ 2

CHERISHING STUDENTS' MEANINGS WHILE SEEKING CHANGE
Walking an Ethical Tightrope

P. Karen Murphy and Patricia A. Alexander

We may have to reflect more deeply than we have, however, about how we can cherish the integrity of the meanings children make and the intuitions they share, while intentionally educating them—or learning along with them—to interpret and to cope with the mystified, endangered world.

— Greene, 1995, p. 48

Chapter Overview

- What do I believe and how does this influence my teaching?
- How do I balance students' perspectives with my intentions to "grow" their understandings?
- What are the tenets underlying persuasive pedagogy?

Inspirational Reflection

The issue of ethics is something that we hold very dear. I have taught and conducted research in the area of ethics, and Patricia taught for nearly a decade in public and parochial schools, where she routinely faced ethical dilemmas. Despite these varied experiences as educators, we were unable to conjure a singular experience that adequately captured the major premise we will forward herein. That is, while each experience offered mooring points along our ethical journeys, no one story illustrated the core of our chosen theme. Thus, we turned to our experiences as students and to what James (1911/1997) referred to as "happenings" with mutual friends, many of whom are noted scholars.

For example, both of us have been heavily influenced by our mentor and friend John J. McDermott (1986) and his teachings and writings about the American experience, cultural identity, and pragmatism, as well as by Maxine Greene's (1995) work on education, art, and social change. Thus, we drew our inspirational reflection from McDermott's take on a classic allegory, and we relied heavily on Greene's work for insight when we considered the ethical implications of teaching for change.

In Book VII of the *Republic* (Plato, n.d./1961), Plato introduces an allegory to describe his understanding of the human condition. In the allegory, individuals have been housed since birth in a subterranean cavern with a long entrance open to the light along its entire width. These individuals are prisoners fettered at the legs and neck so that they cannot turn their heads and are only able to look forward at the wall in front of them. Light glows from a burning fire higher up and at a distance beyond the cave opening, and between the fire and the prisoners, is a parapet upon which puppeteers display a variety of marionettes. The shadows of the marionettes are projected onto the wall in front of the prisoners. The tops of other implements, people, and animals are similarly projected onto the wall as they cross the parapet. Given the circumstances of their imprisonment since birth, these individuals take the images as real—so much so that they make games of naming the images and seeing which prisoner can name the object the fastest.

One of the prisoners unexpectedly breaks free from the chains and ascends to the surface. At the surface, he is blinded by the light of the sun, and some time passes before the figures aboveground come into focus. What he sees is a world very different from the shadows on the wall of the cave, and immediately he feels the need to share his newfound knowledge of the sensible world with his fellow prisoners. Returning to the cave, the enlightened prisoner attempts to instruct his fellow prisoners that they see only shadows and that the real world lies beyond the darkness of the cave. The prisoners threaten to kill him if he continues in his attempts to dismantle their worldview. He and his views are silenced.

Within this deceptively simple allegory, there is a great deal of symbolism. The prisoner's breaking free and ascending toward the light can be interpreted as the process and consequence of enlightenment, and the chains can be seen as akin to society and outside influences such as peers or even the media—influences that keep us locked into a myopic vision of the world. What McDermott helped us see was that the cave was a description of our life, friends, job, university, family, schools, or classrooms. In essence, the cave is a metaphor for where we are at any given time, and the most important thing is to know that we are "caved." As McDermott states so eloquently: "The height of self-deception is to think that where we are, what we do, and what we believe is where others are, do, and believe. Worse, we think that this is what others *should* do and believe" (1986, p. 6).

Such are often the trappings of the teacher–student relationship. In classroom situations, the prisoner who breaks free and comes to know the *real* world is much like the classroom teacher—the disseminator of knowledge. In many cases the knowledge comes from scientifically agreed-upon understandings emanating from a particular culture (e.g., science textbooks or psychological studies of study strategies). In other cases, what is taught simply comes from the district-adopted textbook, which may well provide a one-sided or "matter-of-fact" perspective regarding debatable topics (e.g., causes of the Civil War). The students are best represented in the allegory by the prisoners.

Very early in life, children are enrolled in schools in which a particular worldview is shared—the first cave outside the home. This worldview may or may not conflict with other views such as the child's sense experience or home worldview. Take, for instance, the classic example of the day/night cycle. As a regular occurrence, the child visually experiences the sun ascending and descending in her visual field. Subsequently, she is promoted to the third grade, where her teacher informs her that the sun does not ascend *or* descend, but rather the earth's rotation makes it *appear* as though the sun rises and sets. Such attempts by teachers to enlighten students rarely lead to mutiny or life threats as in Plato's allegory. Indeed, the greater threat is that they lead to skeptical or disengaged learners who hold the knowledge disseminated by the teacher in abeyance (Chinn & Brewer, 1993). In fact, in our own work, students often describe knowledge as the "stuff taught in schools—stuff that lacks value." The teacher's enlightened views conflict with what the child holds to be true, that is, the child's sense of reality.

Within this chapter, what we hope to share is that good pedagogy is necessarily a process involving change and enlightenment—a shedding of light on the shadows of the cave. The ethical conundrum pertains to the careful balancing of the integrity of students' meanings while intentionally teaching so as to potentially alter their knowledge and beliefs. In our research and teaching, we have referred to this process as persuasive pedagogy (Fives & Alexander, 2001; Murphy, 2001). Our intention is to discuss this perspective on maintaining such balance in classroom practice. The key, we believe, lies in the discourse and relationships established within classrooms enacting persuasive pedagogy. Unlike the cave setting, in which a single individual believed himself to be embodied with truth and charged with its dissemination, we will encourage a more reciprocal discourse that relies on evidence and justification by teachers and students, and a relational structure in which students are equipped to consider and defend their perspectives.

Challenges Related to Ethical Decision Making

As teachers, we face a number of challenges when it comes to making decisions about the pedagogical practices we employ in our classrooms. In our teaching, we utilize what we have referred to elsewhere as persuasive pedagogy (Murphy, 2001). What we mean by persuasive pedagogy is captured nicely in Scheffler's writings on knowledge, beliefs, and teaching in which he discusses the special connections between rational explanation, critical dialogue, and teaching, that is, "giving honest reasons and welcoming radical questions."

> In teaching, the teacher is revealing his reasons for the beliefs he wants to transmit and is thus, in effect, submitting his own judgment to the critical scrutiny and evaluation of the student; he is fully engaged in the dialogue by which he hopes to teach, and is thus risking his own beliefs, in lesser or greater degree, as he teaches. (1965, p. 11)

We hold strongly that there is more to teaching than the dissemination of factual knowledge. Like Scheffler, we hold that teaching involves the intentional alteration of the knowledge and beliefs of the students *and* the teacher. That is, in the critical dialogue, both the freed prisoner and the fettered prisoners play a role in teaching and learning. Enacting such a pedagogy means that teachers must face a number of tough questions—questions clearly laced with ethical considerations. Among those questions are: (a) What do I believe? (b) How do I balance students' perspectives with my intentions to "grow" their understandings? and (c) How do teachers and students make sense of the grays where knowledge is rarely considered absolute truth?

Teachers' Beliefs

Knowledge can be thought of as all that is accepted as true that can be externally verified and can be confirmed by others on repeated interactions with the object (i.e., facts; Murphy & Mason, 2006). By comparison, we use the term "belief" to refer to all that one accepts as or wants to be true without the need for verification (e.g., opinions). For example, a teacher may think that students learn best through multiple modalities or that phonics should be used as the primary approach to teaching reading. What is particularly important about beliefs is that individuals attribute a valence of importance to them and are generally prepared to act on what they believe, even in the face of conflicting evidence (e.g., Lord, Ross, & Lepper, 1979). We spend a great deal of time considering our own beliefs about pedagogical choices, ranging from the kinds of texts we choose to instructional activities or assessments. Each of these practices is guided by our beliefs about teaching and learning, and consequently impacts the students we teach.

Balancing Students' Perspectives While Intentionally Educating

There are many teachers who would contend that they are not in the business of altering students' beliefs (Sinatra & Kardash, 2004). Rather, the role of the teacher is to share or disseminate factual, agreed-upon morsels of knowledge. The difficulty, however, is that there is a burgeoning literature suggesting that the beliefs that students bring into the classroom play a powerful role in what they learn over and above the influence of the factual knowledge they possess on a given topic (e.g., Murphy & Alexander, 2004). This is due, in part, to the fact that individuals generally fight to hold on to their beliefs, even in the face of contradictory evidence.

Given that such beliefs can hinder learning, it is imperative that students' beliefs about content-related topics be engaged within the classroom environment in a way that makes them explicit and, potentially, open to modification. In attempting to alter students' beliefs, however, we need to heed McDermott's (1986) admonition. In short, teachers should not be so filled with hubris as to think that they know *the* way that a student *should* believe. Persuasive pedagogy requires teachers to walk a tightrope between embracing students' preconceived beliefs about content understandings and intentionally trying to educate them. The goal is not to get students to respond verbally in a way that aligns with what we hold as teachers but to engage them in rational explanation and critical dialogue both about what they believe and about what we are trying to teach them.

Living in the Gray

The simplicity of a teacher-as-knowledge-disseminator model is that it presupposes that there exists *a* knowledge that students need to possess and that any information that contradicts such knowledge is incorrect. This type of knowledge is often closely associated with truth. Such a position is a comfortable one for teachers in that they can rely heavily on a single source for understanding, with the underlying assumption that all sources would offer the same information. To the contrary, our notion of persuasive pedagogy is situated within a truth-until-further-notice perspective.

That is, the evidence that we use to support, for example, a scientific finding about the benefits of drinking red wine is viable only until we have sufficient evidence to support contradictory hypotheses. As Scheffler (1965) notes, what this means is that teachers' beliefs about what they are sharing with students need to be just as open to scrutiny as the beliefs of the students they teach. For teachers, the quandary surrounds the ease with which they or their students can deal with the grays pedagogically, cognitively, developmentally, culturally, or emotionally. Living in the grays has forced us to think far more deeply about our beliefs and knowledge in relation to the content we teach.

Ethical Teaching Strategies

What we know is that teachers and students possess fairly sophisticated, locally coherent knowledge and belief systems that they employ in thinking about situations, concepts, or problems (Vosniadou, 1994). We also know that such understandings are mediated by the discourse practices, tools, and signs of the local classroom (Kelly & Green, 1998). More important, when teachers' and students' personal theories are challenged, they fight to retain those theories. Although many educational stakeholders would view this as a constraint on good pedagogy, we contend, as we have mentioned previously, that classroom instruction may be reoriented to capitalize on teachers' and students' passions for their understandings through persuasive pedagogy.

In our teaching, we found it useful to delineate the acts that should be evident in our instruction if we are enacting persuasive pedagogy (Murphy, in press). Owing to space limitations, we cannot consider those acts in detail. However, these pedagogical acts are discussed elsewhere, and we share those informative resources at the end of this chapter. In brief, those acts manifest in persuasive pedagogy include the following:

- embracing learning as a change in students' beliefs and knowledge;
- acknowledging and valuing the percepts (feelings) and concepts (ideas) that learners bring to the classroom environment;
- encouraging students to analyze their beliefs critically in relation to what and how teachers teach;
- helping students make their content-relevant knowledge and beliefs explicit;
- recognizing the power of messages in shaping teachers' and students' understandings;
- emphasizing that there is no singular view or understanding of complex concepts and that competing views are worthy of exploration;
- accepting personal *and* scientific evidence as sources of justification;
- assuming that deep-seated changes in students' understandings come from reaching into the social/cultural, motivational, developmental, as well as cognitive realms; and
- valuing the power of rational explanation and critical discourse in teaching and learning.

Synthesis of Ethical Lessons Learned

Just as the freed prisoner felt compelled to share his enlightened perspectives on the world with his fellow prisoners, so we as educators feel duty-bound to share our understandings with the students we teach. Indeed, change lies at the heart of teaching and learning. The difficulty, of course, is that our understandings comprise what we know *and* believe about teaching, learning, and the content of the educational enterprise. As such, our understandings are value laden and necessarily represent a perspective that may not align with the lived experiences of our students. What's more, it would be virtually impossible for teachers to know how their perspectives will align with those of their students a priori.

Consequently, we hold that it is imperative that teachers think more deeply about what it means to teach and to learn, and that they allow for the possible reconceptualization of teaching as a persuasive process. By that we mean a process through which teachers make their beliefs about the content they are teaching explicit to their students and open their ideas to the critical judgment of learners in their classrooms. Similarly, teachers must equip students with the skills needed to think rationally and analytically about their own beliefs and those gleaned from sources of authority, including their teacher. This will enable students to develop the skills needed to examine critically what is being taught not only in the classrooms in which they belong but also in our information-dense society, where evidence and justification are often buried beneath opinion and rhetoric. Teachers have no choice but to walk the tightrope between the meanings a student makes from the world and their duty to intentionally alter those meanings. In fact, the growth and development of our students and our pedagogy depend on it.

Questions for Consideration

Think about what you believe is the goal of teaching. To what extent do you think changing students' knowledge *and* beliefs is important in teaching?

To what extent does "certainty" play a role in your teaching? Are you the sole source of authority? If so, how might this affect your students' learning?

Changing the way one teaches is often a daunting endeavor. What are some ways that you could move your classroom toward one that more closely adheres to the tenets of persuasive pedagogy shared in the chapter?

Supplementary Resources

The Theory and Practice of Persuasive Pedagogy: Murphy, P. K. (Ed.). (2001). Teaching as persuasion: A new metaphor for a new decade. [Special Issue] *Theory into Practice, 40,* 222–278. This special issue of *Theory into Practice* takes a serious look at the underpinnings of persuasive pedagogy. Noted scholars such as Cyndie Hynd and Donna Alvermann consider the extent to which, and under what circumstances, teaching as persuasion is a viable metaphor. Moreover, several examples are offered of persuasive pedagogy in action in classrooms.

Opening Children's Eyes beyond Their Own Experiences: Greene, M. (1995). *Releasing the imagination: Essays on education, the arts, and social change.* San Francisco, CA: Jossey-Bass. This text is just one of Greene's many compelling and inspiring works on education, art, and social change. In the text, she speaks to all educational stakeholders regarding our charge as members of the educational community— that is, to help children imagine a world that is beyond their lived experiences, where there is critical dialogue and the cultivation of new realties, especially given the extent of poverty and desperation in which some children exist.

Integrating Critical/Analytical Discourse in Classrooms: Lipman, M., & Sharp, A. M. (1980). Can moral education be divorced from philosophical inquiry? *Viewpoints in Teaching and Learning, 56*(4), 1–31. Philosophy for Children (P4C) is an approach to classroom discourse whose goal is to foster strong reasoning skills in students and congruence between thought and action. P4C is based on the notion that logic and creativity go hand in hand and that logic does not always suffice as a means of resolving complex human problems. Complete sets of teaching materials, including narrative novels, are available for use in classroom discussions.

References

Chinn, C. A., & Brewer, W. F. (1993). The role of anomalous data in knowledge acquisition: A theoretical framework and implications for science instruction. *Review of Educational Research, 63,* 1–49.

Fives, H., & Alexander, P. A. (2001). Persuasion as a metaphor for teaching: A case in point. *Theory into Practice, 40,* 242–248.

Greene, M. (1995). *Releasing the imagination: Essays on education, the arts, and social change.* San Francisco, CA: Jossey-Bass.

James, W. (1911/1997). The meaning of the word truth. In W. James (Ed.), *The meaning of truth* (pp. 217–220). Amherst, NY: Prometheus Books. (Originally published 1911.)

Kelly, G. J., & Green, J. (1998). The social nature of knowing: Toward a socio-cultural perspective on conceptual change and knowledge construction. In B. Guzzetti & C. Hynd (Eds.), *Perspectives on conceptual change: Multiple ways to understand knowing and learning in a complex world* (pp. 145–181). Mahwah, NJ: Lawrence Erlbaum Associates.

Lord, C. G., Ross, L., & Lepper, M. R. (1979). Biased assimilation and attitude polarization: The effects of prior theories on subsequently considered evidence. *Journal of Personality and Social Psychology, 37*, 2098–2109.

McDermott, J. J. (1986). *Streams of experience: Reflections on the history and philosophy of American culture.* Amherst, MA: University of Massachusetts Press.

Murphy, P. K. (2001). Persuasive pedagogy: A new metaphor for a new decade. *Theory into Practice, 40*, 224–227.

Murphy, P. K. (in press). The eye of the beholder: The interplay of social and cognitive components in change. *Educational Psychologist.*

Murphy, P. K., & Alexander, P. A. (2004). Persuasion as a dynamic multi-dimensional process: An investigation of individual differences and intra-individual differences. *American Educational Research Association, 41*, 337–363.

Murphy, P. K., & Mason, L. (2006). Changing knowledge and beliefs. In P. A. Alexander & P. Winne (Eds.), *Handbook of Educational Psychology* (2nd ed.) (305-324). Mahwah, NJ: Lawrence Erlbaum.

Plato. (1961). *Republic.* (Lane Cooper, Trans.). In E. Hamilton & H. Cairns (Eds.), *The collected dialogues of Plato: Including the letters* (575-844). New York: Pantheon Books. (Original work n.d.).

Scheffler, I. (1965). *Conditions of knowledge.* Chicago: University of Chicago Press.

Sinatra, G. M., & Kardash, C. M. (2004). Teacher candidates' epistemological beliefs, dispositions, and views on persuasive pedagogy. *Contemporary Educational Psychology, 29*, 483–498.

Vosniadou, S. (1994). Capturing and modeling the process of conceptual change. *Learning and Instruction, 4*, 45–69.

KNOW THYSELF
Perceptions Based on Society, Ethnicity, and Experience

Joanne Kilgour Dowdy

The question is not what you look at, but what you see.

—*Henry David Thoreau*

Chapter Overview

- A Caribbean woman's perspective on education in the United States of America.
- Learning to teach from a culturally responsive perspective.
- Being a teacher/learner in the space of an ethical classroom.

Inspirational Reflection

Two things I am really sure about. One, I am not a revolutionary; two, I am not black American. These two things, among others, became clear to me when I was teaching in Harlem, just out of the training program at Teachers College, Columbia University. The first idea came to me like a bolt of lightning when I read the autobiography of Malcolm X. Malcolm X was serious about his religion, committed to honesty, and loyal to Elijah Muhammad. These three choices cost him his life. I had no such commitment to anything that I could name or dream of in my life up to that point. The question of being ethical as a teacher and human being was another matter.

The next thing that I knew after teaching in Harlem and realizing that there was a cultural context that produced Malcolm X, a gray shadow in my consciousness, was that I would never be able to reference that community experience. I barely knew how to go to and leave from the school in Harlem from and to the home I shared with my host family in mid-Manhattan. Talk about different worlds. I came out of the Juilliard School and went uptown to the black Mecca of the United States and had to start studying all over again. I had spent four years in a school for artists where I saw only four other black people on a regular basis. The graduate program that trained me to be a teacher, in New York City, had only one other black teacher in one of the classes that I attended during the year I was there. She, also, was an immigrant. I saw her in one class, once a week, for one semester. This happened on a campus just outside the backdoor of Harlem.

So I was not black American, I was Trinidadian. I was Caribbean when it was necessary for me to establish an identity that was non-Jamaican. It seemed very few people whom I met in New York in those seven years that I lived there even knew that there were other islands besides Jamaica and Grenada. Malcolm X's mother was from Grenada. I never hear anyone mention this fact in the much-repeated litanies about his life. How did she get to be with Malcolm X's father? Why did Malcolm X's father resent her because she was better educated than he was and was a light-skinned woman? I do not remember these points being raised in any discussion that I have been privy to during my stint in New York or since leaving it seventeen years ago.

I remember telling my brother these facts when we were discussing Malcolm X's journey to becoming a minister of his own religious organization. I guess I am particularly sensitive to the issue because I am an immigrant who found myself married to a dark-skinned American man who wanted to discard me when I earned one degree more than he had earned. That is one of the reasons I keep Malcolm X's book on my shelf. I know that he knew about stuff that other people do not care to remember. He was brutally honest in his dealings with life.

So it seems to me that the discussion of ethics, the discipline of doing good and avoiding bad, is a good one for someone like me to participate in since I have been through the middle passage of American education. Like the slaves of our history, I left the Caribbean and landed in a state on the eastern coast of these United States. In my new education, as a non-white immigrant, I had to learn what was truth within that context and what I needed to do to maintain my sense of good and bad so that I could live a productive life. I had to learn what were my duty and moral obligation to the students in my classrooms in the face of their believing that I was not born an American and therefore could not possibly have anything to teach them. Herein lies the story of my evolution from provincial black to pan-African community member to world citizen.

In the unfolding tale I hope to share my insights about the ways in which we integrate our settings on a daily basis, whether consciously or not, and discuss the fact that our relationships with our students is soundly situated in the nature of our interactions with them. More important, I want to reveal my awareness of the fact that students and teachers create a theater for learning within their classrooms. In this theater, circumscribed by time, space, and academic goals, the community forms a unit that generates knowledge particular to the values that it comes with. The organism also discovers new values as a community and prepares to go into the world ready to do its duty with a working knowledge of good and bad actions and what it means to live with the consequences of its choices.

The importance of this work, founded on the understanding that teachers pass on important information about their academic and social knowledge, cannot be stressed enough. Without the confidence that comes from knowing that we teachers are valuable to our students, and ultimately to our society, we could not do the hard work that ethical teaching demands. Our students would read us as incompetents within the first minutes of their arrival in our classroom, and we would be doomed to their constant and unflinching disrespect over the time that they spend with us.

My students in Harlem taught me to earn their respect. This lesson was not posted on a bulletin board in the classroom or hallway or school building. The instruction was part of the day-to-day interaction that they designed through spoken, written, or body language codes. They held me to the highest standards of behavior in the face of their insistence that some of them could do what they wanted, when they wanted, and just because they wanted to do their own thing. That was a tough exam to set and an even more difficult one to pass. The students knew this. They were veterans of the academic wars that they had had to participate in as part of an urban school system. They had no time to waste on fake teachers who just needed a paycheck and did not live in their community. What I learned firsthand is that expectations from a teacher set the standard of achievement in a classroom. This fact has not changed for me as I have grown and matured in my philosophy of teaching and learning in the ensuing seventeen years.

Challenges Relating to Ethical Decision Making

Malcolm X's mother held on to her children for as long as she could before the state agency took them away from her home. She ended up in an asylum because of the pain that the separation from her husband and children exacted on her mental and physical health. I know that my mother separated from my father when she finally became too ill to cope with his harsh treatment of her and the effect that it was having on her children. When my mother died, I was eleven years old; she had done all she could to keep her youngest child from the ravages of the poison that is domestic violence. Malcolm X was saved from the ravages of his father's wrath but not the caustic effects of a racist society that would not forgive him for being black, male, brilliant, and without a mother to love and protect him. Not much is made of that mother's journey as a single woman trying to raise her family in an unforgiving world. Malcolm X, however, made a way out of no way with the help of his sister. People celebrate his rise from notoriety to spiritual liberation. I celebrate the women in his life and the social support system that was intact when he stepped into his life as a leader of a faith community.

In the face of serious challenges to my "taken for granted" notions about what should happen in schools for black children and other non-white students, and about the way that teachers should relate to students, I had to come to terms with the reality of being a minority in a minority community when I arrived in New York City. In Trinidad, where I was born and lived until I was twenty-two, I was raised in the equivalent of parochial schools. The Catholic Church was the organizing agent in my life and in the lives of the students who went to primary and secondary school within that system. We went to church twice a week when we were in grade school. In high school we could expect to take part in discussions of the Catholic faith once a week and sit in a church function at least once a month. Some of the students in my class were members of the Hindu or Muslim faith. Their faith was never discussed in all the years that I was a student in the school system in my first country. The silence on the backgrounds of these children has been a constant reminder to me that I am not the center of the universe.

What happens when the teacher's faith community is different from her students' faith community? Since we do not talk about religion in public schools in the United States, at least not officially, it leaves one less space in which teachers and their students can build a safe zone for their relationship to grow. The taboo subject of religious culture may become a wall between possible allies. In my experiences across the five states where I have lived and taught for twenty years in this country, I have not been able to use any faith community as a means of coalition building in my classroom. I mourn the absence of that option in my teaching toolkit because I am a product of a faith community and its value of education. Malcolm X was a product of a faith community. The black community in most of the schools where I have taught relies heavily on its faith communities.

Because I am considered black, and sometimes mistaken for a black American until I open my mouth, my colleagues in public schools and academia have projected their ideas about the faith community that raised me onto their relationships with me. I have sometimes been received with shock in faculty meetings, dissertation committees, and social outings for faculty when I disclose my Catholic upbringing in parochial schools. These experiences have led me to consider what kind of projections I must be passing on to my students because I have preconceived notions about their faith communities or lack any idea about their culture of faith and the value that these groups place on the education of young people.

In Harlem I met parents who came to meetings that I called and let me know in no uncertain terms that the teacher was the law in the classroom and if their child could not meet the standards set down by that authority, then said minor would be seriously chastised and disciplined by the parent in question. This was different from the stereotypes that I had been fed while I was preparing to teach as a student coming out of a graduate teachers program down the street from the school. It was not the reality painted in movies, television shows, and magazines. I had to grow into the knowledge that every child has a parent, or a family member, who is supporting them in their journey to become educated and to take their place in society as a productive citizen. This support system may not look like the extended family network that I had when my mother died and her mother and siblings took over my care and comfort. But the will to grow a person is there in every community, and I learned that teachers have to become alert to the signs that indicate the level of that input for the child's well-being.

This awareness of the social network that operates in every person's life, seen or unseen, has affected the way that I set up my research studies. I always ask participants to direct me to the nearest and dearest people in their lives so that I can get second and third perspectives on the participant I am writing about. I always share video and audio cassettes of interviews with each participant, and a transcript of the interview, so that they can see and read the product of our interaction for the study. If there are any problems with the results of my interviews, the participants get a chance to pull me up short as soon as they view themselves on tape and paper. They can ask to have comments edited or removed from the files. Both of us, participant and interviewer, build a bridge of understanding over the interview transcript and come to new understandings of our work as a team.

Ethical Teaching Strategies

The strategies that I learned to handle difficult situations regarding my duty of good behavior in my classrooms and research projects may have a direct link to the exposure that I had to the idea of community. The questions of what makes a community and how we perform as ethical members of a community have been constant themes in my evolution as a teacher/leader/

activist/artist/student. I do projects in my classroom that remind students that as teachers they are going to have to find ways to "build up" their own students. I learn about these preservice teachers by asking them to choose articles from the daily papers that interest them and putting these clippings into folders so that I can study their choices and begin to add to their folders with other clippings that I find in magazines and other publications. I am on a quest to build bridges to the students who people my classrooms.

I also ask the teachers to bring in poems that they can share with the class. My hope is to hear their inner voices and learn from the stories that these poems tell. It is another way to enter a "faith community" that is hidden from the daily routines that formal academic settings force us to maintain. In a way, it is the underbelly of teaching that gets to the heart of relationships. This fabric of community must be carefully stitched together as teachers and students build bridges to and from their different worlds.

When I get to know my students I have to be able to handle the stories that they bring to the classroom. Their lives, their challenges, their personal dilemmas loom large as they begin to build trust. They learn about my trials and frustrations and the kind of care that I present to them as a co-learner in our journey along the path of formal education. I believe that I learned to do this delicate ballet of seek and discern in my student teaching days in Harlem. Malik was one of the students who taught me how to stand upright in the face of serious provocation. He won my heart in his serious talent as a writer. Then he broke my heart when I came to know that he was sent "upstate" because he broke the law. I learned right then to take the truth as a lesson and to use it to be more fully aware of the world.

When Gregory, in the ninth grade, threw a full bag of books at me, and almost hit me, I had a rude awakening to the level of anger of some students in my classroom. That incident taught me to stand up for myself in an environment that took this kind of student behavior as just another incident in paradise. Greg, a fictitious name, was transferred to another school. I returned to my classroom, and the students seemed to show me a slightly different kind of respect than I had received before that unfortunate confrontation. His friends did not taunt me or make life unlivable during the last months of the semester, even though they were upset that their friend was put out of the school. The families who knew that the boy in question had been a troubled child since he was in grade school were relieved to know that their own children would not be intimidated by this youngster's angry outbursts any longer. If I had allowed myself to be dominated by the stereotypes that I had been fed by the media and schools where I had studied before becoming a teacher, I would not have been able to accept the level of concern that the teachers and parents at that school expressed during those difficult months. No one wanted a casualty of the system to be laid on their doorsteps. Everyone worked hard to keep that young man in school and restore me to my place in the classroom.

The ability to ask difficult questions and follow the lead to the answers is part of the legacy of Malcolm X. I saw this culture laid bare in the school where I did my student teaching and spent my first year as a licensed teacher. My supervising teacher during the first three months at the school was a community mother, and she made sure that she let the other teachers know that I was her ward. If there was any trouble with me, she was to be consulted about the facts and the next steps to be considered. She had my back. That is a role model for me and my student teachers. The importance of the extended family in the lives of young urban students is invaluable. Teachers cut out a huge part of their possibility of succeeding with this population when they discount or deem invisible the hands that feed, clothe, direct, nurture, and monitor the youth who come to their classrooms every day.

While I was teaching my students in Harlem to be proud of their heritage as black people, descendants of Africans and the soul of their country, I learned to understand some of the brilliance of Malcolm X's speeches in their powers of persuasion and their use of the vernacular. I started to have a glimpse of what the fire in him represented. My heart began to read Malcolm X for the power that his tongue brought to him. This journey made me more aware that I was still singing my Caribbean song in a strange land, just as Bob Marley told us. And like Grace Marie, who described her language experience in her poem "June Plum Rooting" (Dowdy, 2005), I learned that I liked the taste in my mouth when I spoke my tongue:

> Say this, not dat.
> They can't hear mi when my sound sings like the breeze
> Kissing longingly bamboo leaves
> Or, when sugar cane spills sweet
> From the corners of mi island mouthpiece. (p. 1)

My love and valuing of my language helped me to lead my students to a celebration of their love of language. I encouraged them to ask hard questions about themselves and their history and the future that they wanted to build. The answers were sometimes disturbing. But Malcolm X had a legacy of asking hard questions and looking for the answers. That's what got him into a difficult situation with the Nation of Islam. That's what cost him his life when he stood up on his own two feet and declared truth as he saw it. Right? At least, that's my reading of the book and the way that I passed on the message to my students in those classes I taught in Harlem. That's the very reason I still keep the autobiography on my bookshelf. The only way to keep Malcolm X's spirit alive is to insist on facing the harsh realities with a confidence that the truth will be a far better situation than living in a lie.

Synthesis of Ethical Lessons Learned

I was talking with my friend about the meaning of Malcolm X in my life and it occurred to me that I really would not be able to write anything about this topic at all if it were not for my brother and his interest in books. More important, if Malcolm X's life story was not written down, I would never have heard about him in Trinidad. The power of the word was significant to those of us who lived outside the United States. We needed Alex Haley (1966) to get the story down on paper so that we could learn about this black man who turned the United States on its head. How wonderful that Malcolm X's community supported and nourished him at every stage of his development. Thank God for Alex Haley and his reporter's curiosity. Thanks to the divine timing that let Malcolm X and Alex Haley get together when they did. Through that collaboration we can begin to see how history facilitated the blossoming of a new consciousness in the land that made both those men.

Finally, Malcolm X's willingness to travel outside the country and join his fellow Muslims in Mecca is a sign that I have done the right thing by leaving my original home in the Caribbean and coming to be with my fellow humans in the African diaspora. Regardless of the difficulties that I have encountered along the way to finding a language that helps me communicate with my black American family and the wider society, I know that we are kin. No amount of cultural expressions or historical baggage caused by the middle-passage trauma can erase the essence of who we are as a family. The DNA of all humans is African. We have no control over what we look like. Malcolm X saw that when he got to Mecca and sat among Muslims of every description. He understood that God is One; men call Him variously.

This is an important value to uphold when you are a teacher. Regardless of the physical appearance of my students, I look on them as members of my family. Of course, all families have issues with certain members of their tribe. The important thing that has to be borne in mind when dealing with these difficult people is that there is always someone who can appeal to them. That is the value of the network within a community. Someone knows somebody who can call on something that will have a constructive effect on the matter at hand. I carry that lesson from Harlem in me and apply it in all my relationships. The most unbecoming students or parents have a support system that can be called into play when the situation demands a third party to intervene.

I like to be reminded of that scene in Spike Lee's film *Malcolm X* where the inside of the mosque is shown. I bet that the whole camera crew and actors on that set had a serious revolution of spirit when they stood inside that spiritual space. It is just like Malcolm X to make us throw off our cultural shackles and step up to the plate of some serious change: mind, soul, and heart. That is my Malcolm X, as my grandmother would say about one of her grandchildren acting out and showing their "nature." She would shake her head and smile at the chaos some tot was causing in the ordered life of the adults around her. Malcolm X did the same thing with the adults around him—shook up their world and caused them to look with new eyes at the life in which they were involved. Just like his daddy, Malcolm X showed those around him that God does not sleep; she just puts on pajamas and looks on as we human beings learn to get along.

My students in Harlem rearranged my preconceived notions about them and caused me to put aside the stereotypes about black Americans about which my Eurocentric college education had deluded me. The so-called bad students, usually the ones who were bored to death with the rote learning that they were forced to endure in the public schools, made me pay attention to the value of an arts-based approach to teaching and learning across all ages and disciplines. This is a cornerstone of my teaching philosophy to this day.

And so the story of learning to "see" continues with me and my white, undergraduate, mostly Christian students out here in the Midwest. We show our nature to each other and find out that we are not so different after all. Not even with me showing up with my nappy hair hanging out and them finding a safe place to tell me about their "hillbilly" roots or the "redneck" in their family whom they never, never told anyone about before coming into my classroom to learn about pumping up reading and writing in adolescence and adulthood. Is that not an important lesson for both sides, teacher and student, to learn from each other? I think so. In fact, I know so. I celebrate our diversity every time I step into that classroom and look into those white faces that come from German, Dutch, Native American, African, Mexican, Croatian, or Polish roots. I sing America, just like Langston Hughes wrote, and my students continue to teach me how to do that.

I work to uphold that value system of seeing beyond the surface of people's lives in my research. My years of learning to build community in the classroom have taught me to listen for the undertone of the stories that people share with me when I ask them to tell me about their journey in formal education circles. Rather than focus on the "traditional" outcomes that represent success, including entrance to prestigious academic institutions and winning prizes in school competitions, I look for the learning curve that each participant represents. My interest in the diversity of paths that lead to a sense of success and confidence in the learner makes it possible to see and hear the richness of each community. Like the jeweler who discovered a diamond buried on the bank of a river, the one that everyone else treated like a tree stump and used to clean the dirt off their feet before entering the water, I look beneath the surface and dig out the precious gems of history from each person whom I interview and write about.

Questions for Consideration

Think about the time when you were the "only" something in a group in a new setting—the only mother, the only Jew, the only person with diabetes or another medical condition, the only immigrant among North Americans. What did you do to make a connection with the people in the group? What did someone in the group do to reach out to you? How would you use this experience to make relationships with your students in your classroom?

What would you do about the fact that some of the issues that your students reveal to you concerning their family, living conditions, or personal dilemmas affect the way that they relate to others in the classroom, especially since you cannot reveal the background information that you know about them? Can you find a way to include the students in the problem-solving journey?

When you come to realize the terms that students use to describe you (i.e., some people call Caribbean immigrants "monkey catchers" or "nimmigrants"), do you talk about these issues in a group discussion or do you talk with students individually when they use these references or laugh at jokes that use them? Are you willing to talk about the times when you were the butt of some unkind jokes because of your sex, race, class, or ethnic background?

Supplementary Resources

Overcoming Teacher Biases toward Children: Ladson-Billings, G. (1997). *The dreamkeepers: Successful Teachers of African American children.* San Francisco, CA: Jossey-Bass. This book "integrates scholarly research with stories of eight successful teachers in a predominantly African American school district to illustrate that the 'dream' of all teachers and parents—academic success for all children—is alive and can be emulated." Teachers share successes and plans and prospects for improving the school experiences of African American students.

Exemplary Teachers' Teaching Strategies in Multicultural Settings: Willis, A. I., Garcia, G. E., Barrera, R., & Harris, V. J. (Eds.). (2003).

Multicultural issues in literacy research and practice. Mahwah, NJ: Lawrence Erlbaum Associates. It is the responsibility of teachers to find out the backgrounds of their students and develop teaching strategies that are culturally appropriate for their advancement in academic settings. The highest ethical standards must be recognized and pursued in the venture of educating young minds. The approaches to the diverse communities used by these teachers represent the ideal of ethical teaching in context. Teachers will get ideas about the ways in which they can tap their community for resources and experts who can be brought into the classroom.

Exemplary Educators' Ethical Approaches to Language Issues: Delpit, L., & Dowdy, J. K. (Eds.). (2002). *The skin that we speak: Thoughts on language and culture in the classroom.* New York: New Press. Use these essays by people who have had to climb the language mountain to communicate effectively in diverse settings. These discussions help to establish the context for understanding ethical lessons about living in an effective community and dealing with life's challenges. Teachers of all age groups can use these topics as conversation starters on ethical topics.

References

Dowdy, J. K. (2005). "Introduction." In J. K. Dowdy (Ed.), *Readers of the quilt: Essays on being black, female and literate* (pp. 1–11). Cresskill, NJ: Hampton Press.

Haley, A. (1966). *The autobiography of Malcolm X by Malcolm (As told to Alex Haley).* New York: Grove Press.

✂ 4

DEFINING THE UNSPOKEN RULES
The Ethical Practices

Ying Tang

Impairment—An interference in professional functioning that is reflected in one or more of the following ways: (a) an inability and/or unwillingness to acquire and integrate professional standards into one's repertoire of professional behavior; (b) an inability to acquire professional skills to reach an acceptable level of competency; (c) an inability to control personal stress, psychological dysfunction and/or excessive emotional reactions that interfere with professional functioning.

—Lamb et al., 1987, p. 598

Chapter Overview

- Responsibilities of an ethical counselor–educator when dealing with issues relating to student impairment.
- How educators should approach impaired students regarding their well-being and professional competency.
- Recommended admission and evaluation policies and procedures for educators in higher education programs.

Inspirational Reflection

In an ideal world, it makes perfect sense that educators should deal only with issues that are academic. As educators, we want every student to succeed and we expect them to work hard for their success. We should never need to worry about advising students who are psychologically disturbed or even suicidal. However, we do not live in a perfect world, and we do encounter students who seem to be deeply affected by a variety of personal, medical, and psychological problems and difficulties. Unfortunately, when it comes to working with students whose performance has been impaired for a variety of reasons,

I have to admit that the greatest difficulty educators encounter is often not the academic situation but their ethical responsibilities. On the one hand, we hope for the best for every student; on the other, we find ourselves struggling to find ways to communicate our deepest concerns regarding the well-being and the professional competency of certain individuals. Especially for teacher and counselor education programs, the dilemma lies in differentiating between the educators' responsibility to serve the individuals and to protect the children or clients who will be affected in the future once the impaired individuals start working as professionals.

The term "impairment" began to be used within the field of psychology to capture a broad range of situations involving deficiencies in professional performance in the 1970s (Kempthorne, 1979). This broad range related to impairment includes substance abuse, mental illness, and physical and emotional limitations. I have had experience working with students whose ability to counsel was impaired by their emotional or medical problems. I often utilize supervisory feedback to communicate my concerns. I cannot stress enough the importance of raising students' self-awareness and providing supervisory feedback in an education program. It is essential for the development of the trainees that they are carefully guided to reflect, explore, and analyze themselves so they can recognize any distortions, denial, or other personal defense mechanisms that might play a role in their unconstructive behaviors or poor professional performance. Having a healthy self-awareness can only enhance the work of teachers and counselors, making them aware of who they are so they will not hide behind their profession and abuse their power to take advantage of their students/clients.

Critical yet supportive supervisory feedback is one effective way to raise trainees' self-awareness. Without timely and appropriate supervisory feedback, students cannot begin the process of self-improvement. Students' ability to receive and incorporate feedback is essential for their professional development. As an educator and supervisor dealing with struggling students, my concern is always about their ability to perform required tasks or to achieve the required level of competency. Students need to know that no one is perfect and that we all have blind spots when it comes to identifying our weaknesses, and sometimes even our strengths. However, supervisory feedback, sometimes known as "constructive criticism," is hard to receive. Most students know and are reminded that the purpose of feedback is not to criticize their performance but to help them improve.

Unfortunately, certain individuals cannot handle any negative feedback and they feel offended, become defensive, or even completely shut down and dismiss any further feedback. For a counseling profession that emphasizes and values human characteristics such as genuineness, caring, and openness, I find such inappropriate reactions to be troublesome. I had a student whose cognitive functioning was impaired by a medical condition, and he struggled in all the skill-based classes he took. However, he was determined and believed that if he could study harder and practice the counseling skills more often, he could become a competent counselor. Having dealt with such students, I have not only had to balance my ethical and legal responsibilities but have also found myself battling with students' denial, defensiveness, and passive–aggressive behaviors. Needless to say, the process of dealing with impairment is one of the most complex and stressful problems an educator can face.

Challenges Relating to Ethical Decision Making

There are several reasons I am so concerned about trainees' impairment and potential harm to their students or clients. First, the professional counseling ethical mandate of non-maleficence (Kitchener, 2000), or "doing no harm," demands that the client's welfare be the counselor's first and foremost concern. The Code of Ethics and Standards of Practice of the American Counseling Association (ACA) requires counselors to "refrain from offering . . . professional services when their physical, mental or emotional problems are likely to harm a client" (2005, Section C.2.g). The National Education Association's Code of Ethics of the Education Profession (NEA, 1975) also states that an ethical educator should not engage in professional relationships with students for personal gain.

Second, researchers have already proven that a counselor can positively or negatively affect clients depending on the counselor's mental health (Corey, Corey, & Callanan, 1993). I do not believe individuals can effectively counsel or teach if they are not able to master the required skills or when they are busy battling their own demons. I do embrace how gestalt theory (Corey, 2004) defined capable counseling—you help others more efficiently when you are being real about who you are. I believe the learning process begins when students are willing to learn and when they allow the delivery of the information through various formats. When I teach, I like to assess and make connections to three dimensions of a person (i.e., the cognitive, affective, and behavioral). In my opinion, blockages in receiving information and self-defeating paralyzing behavior in the classroom, if unaddressed, are likely to be exacerbated in professional work after graduation.

Third, there are legal implications when impaired student trainees cause harm as a result of incompetence, abuse, or negligence. In addition to the fact that students will be liable and subject to malpractice suits, the supervising faculty members as well as the institution may also be held accountable for the students' malpractice. Since I am one of the field-experience supervisors in my program, the responsibility to ensure the ethical and legal protection of both clients' and student trainees' rights is always on my mind when I teach and supervise students.

One of the challenges that I have found is that, under normal circumstances, students or trainees who suffer from any mental or physical problems would rather keep them to themselves than openly discuss them or inform educators. Since the relationship, communication, and interaction between an educator and students are often limited to being professional, it is common that the educator is not able to identify the problem until the troubled individual is well into the program or has already gone into field-experience training. Subsequently, it is much too late when the student's deficiencies become obvious and the problems manifest themselves into an "impairment" before educators can provide critical and timely feedback or refer the student for counseling or therapy. As a department, all faculty members are well aware of the problem and we work hard together to find solutions to how we can establish an early identification mechanism in our program so we can assist and advise students at the first sign of a problem. This experience helped me realize that I am not alone in the decision-making process. Through consultation, communication, and cooperation among faculty members, the potential risk of misjudgment or even a lawsuit could be significantly reduced.

Another challenge that I face has been how to approach and confront students who are not making adequate professional progress and have not responded to feedback. I often fall back on classroom evaluations, which include content assessment, observation of skills, and reflective writing. Needless to say, a fair and ethical decision should not rely solely on the classroom assessments, nor should I be the only faculty confronting the student. To be an ethical educator, I often self-monitor by asking myself questions such as "Am I being too hard on the student?," "Have I provided enough support and feedback so the student can improve?," and "Have I given the individual enough time to improve?" In addition to self-monitoring, I ensure constant communication and consultation with other faculty members to voice my concerns and get feedback from them regarding the troubled students. Through cooperative effort, we can not only keep track of the progress of the students but also provide consistent and accurate feedback to them.

Ethical Teaching and Advising Strategies

Since evaluating and supervising students is our professional obligation, most educators would agree that they feel more comfortable when there are clear rules and procedures for appropriate monitoring or dismissal of impaired students. However, researching through several faculty handbooks from different institutions, I discovered it is not uncommon to find minimal or no specific instructions or procedures to assist faculty in evaluating and advising "impaired" student trainees. Consequently, the next best option, in my opinion, is to turn to my colleagues for serious discussion and a series of consultations. Since there are limited resources on the issues of identification and evaluation of trainee impairment (Elman et al., 1999; Forrest et al., 1999; Frame & Stevens-Smith, 1995; Wilkerson, 2006), my colleagues and I gathered information regarding the best practices and appropriate procedures of monitoring students mostly through the ACA's Code of Ethics (2005), professional conferences, personal contacts, a counselor educator listserv, and consultation with other counselor–educators.

On the basis of my experience, I found some students did not react to or even totally dismissed my feedback and thought that I was just "picking on them." More often than not, these students believe that if they can pass the class, they will be fine. I have had one student who was angry, defensive, and even vowed to "never take Dr. Tang's class ever again" and later found herself getting similar supervisory feedback from another faculty member during her field-experience training. In fact, on the basis of the experiences of other educators and professionals who have fought and lost the lawsuits brought against them or their institution by impaired students, one message that is abundantly clear is that interventions made by only one or a few individual faculty are not effective. Research into the limited literature on trainees' impairment shows that a systemic approach right from admission screening to student teaching/internship evaluation is the most recommended approach. Needless to say, if a student has received consistent supervisory feedback from different faculty, the message will be loud and clear that he or she has some work to do. Over the past few years, in my program, we have been adapting suitable procedures, best practices recommendations, and policies from other counselor education programs. We have added a disclosure contract that requires students to abide by the rules and policies of the program, created a new performance appraisal—a disposition survey—added another documenting procedure, and reserved time in our biweekly meetings to address any concern relating to students.

Synthesis of Ethical Lessons Learned

As I mentioned earlier, a systemic approach, from admission screening to student teaching/internship evaluation, is the most practical and effective approach. The first gate-keeping mechanism in our program is the admission process. In addition to the standard graduate program application procedures, we also require all applicants to go through a twenty–thirty minute face-to-face interview with two faculty members. We ask applicants several standard questions and we evaluate them using an interview survey. We take additional notes on the first impressions and hunches that we may have during the brief conversation. The screening process is very helpful in terms of giving us an opportunity to interact with potential candidates. After the interviewing process, the counselor education faculty meet and discuss the results and share notes with one another. However, the admission interview is not perfect, and it is inevitable that some students who are impaired or unsuitable will be admitted to counselor education programs.

The second, and more in-depth, screening process starts during our first semester of course work. We use two evaluations, a midpoint progress report, and a disposition survey, which is meant to serve as an early identification mechanism. The midpoint progress report is designed to document progress and provide formal feedback to students regarding their academic performance in the intro class; it also comments on the student's openness to feedback and willingness to accept personal responsibility for change in academic and non-academic areas. In the skill-based course, faculty evaluate each student on the basis of observations of skill performance, response to supervisory feedback, and reflective writing assignments using a set of ten dispositional attributes. The dispositions include "have a genuine interest in the welfare of others," "open to learning," and "be able to understand the perspective of others." Students are continually evaluated using the same criteria in another skill-based class and eventually in the field-experience class at the end of the master's program. All the evaluations are given to students and filed in the students' academic records. The early identification of problem students allows faculty members to provide additional support or suggest an outside referral and to communicate our concern early in the program, so the feedback is timely for at-risk students who otherwise do not realize that counseling is not the ideal profession for them.

In addition to conducting performance appraisals, faculty review every student on a regular basis at faculty meetings. Any faculty concerns regarding a student or resolution made during the meeting is documented in the minutes. We also have developed a remediation procedure. For any student who continues to struggle either academically or for other reasons, in addition to the feedback he or she receives in class, his or her academic advisor is involved in communicating concerns and meeting with the student to further assess the issue and provide additional support if needed. During the advisement, any concern discussed or recommended remediation is also documented in the candidate consultation report, which is signed by the student. The student keeps a copy of the report and another is filed in the student's record. We have also learned from unforeseen difficulties that we encountered in this ongoing process and have revised our policies on the basis of lessons learned. For example, we have decided a student cannot take a skill-based course more than twice. If a student cannot master the necessary skills after taking the same course twice, we have strong reservations regarding the skill competency of the individual.

Our screening and evaluation strategies are twofold. First, we make sure every student is informed about the rules and assessments that we implement throughout the program. Second, through feedback, oral or written, students are reminded that they are being carefully monitored. Recently, the Division of Education has also revised its policies and procedures on professional competencies, due process, moral character, and fitness for education programs. On the basis of the policy, if a student's performance is unprofessional or unsatisfactory, and if the problem has persisted without improvement, and if additional time in the program will not result in significantly improved performance, the department may recommend to the associate dean that the student be terminated from the program. I feel that our department has taken all the necessary steps to ensure that we hold graduates accountable for their performance, competency, and ethical behaviors. Even though I would be naïve to think that our system and policy are perfect, I do think we have continuously and rigorously to adhere to more secure and adaptive policies to safeguard not only the integrity of our program but also the students who will be served by our graduates.

Questions for Consideration

Reflect on what it means to you to adopt curricular programs based on integrity. What does your school curriculum say about your integrity?

How does it feel when you hear about students who are terminated from a particular program or invited to pursue a different career path?

Screening procedures play an important role in the evaluation of a program's worth and how teachers are held accountable. Do you have adequate and measurable screening programs that are correlated with your assessment outcomes?

Supplementary References

Bemak, F., Epp, L. R., & Keys, S. G. (1999). Impaired graduate students: A process model of graduate program monitoring and intervention. *International Journal for the Advancement of Counseling, 21*(1), 19–30.

Bhat, C. S. (2005). Enhancing counseling gatekeeping with performance appraisal protocols. *International Journal for the Advancement of Counseling, 27*(3), 399–411.

Plymouth State University Counselor Education Program. (n.d.). *Screening and the extended admission process.* Retrieved January 22, 2007, from http://www.plymouth.edu/graduate/counseling/curriculum.html.

These articles provide information regarding the screening and evaluation processes and models used or suggested by other institutions and educators.

References

American Counseling Association. (2005). *Code of ethics and standards of practice.* Alexandria, VA: Author.

Corey, G. (2004). *Theory and practice of group counseling* (6th ed.). Belmont, CA: Wadsworth/Thomson.

Corey, G., Corey, M. S., & Callanan, P. (1993). *Issues and ethics in the helping professions* (4th ed.). Pacific Grove, CA: Brooks/Cole.

Elman, N., Forrest, L., Vacha-Haase, T., & Gizara, S. (1999). A systems perspective on trainee impairment: Continuing the dialogue. *The Counseling Psychologist, 27*(5), 712–721.

Forrest, L., Elman, N., Gizara, S., & Vacha-Haase, T. (1999). Trainee impairment: A review of identification, remediation, dismissal, and legal issues. *The Counseling Psychologist, 27*(5), 627–686.

Frame, M. W., & Stevens-Smith, P. (1995). Out of harm's way: Enhancing monitoring and dismissal processes in counselor education programs. *Counselor Education and Supervision, 35*(2), 118–129.

Kempthorne, G. (1979). The impaired physician: The role of the state medical society. *Wisconsin Medical Journal, 78*, 24–25.

Kitchener, K. S. (2000). *Foundations of ethical practice, research and teaching in psychology.* Mahwah, NJ: Lawrence Erlbaum.

Lamb, D. H., Presser, N. R., Pfost, K. S., Baum, M. C., Jackson, V. R., & Jarvis, P. A. (1987). Confronting professional impairment during the internship: Identification, due process, and remediation. *Professional Psychology: Research and Practice, 18*, 597–603.

National Education Association. (1975). *Code of ethics of the education profession.* Retrieved January 2, 2007, from http://www.nea.org/aboutnea/code.html.

Wilkerson, K. (2006). Impaired students: Applying the therapeutic process model to graduate training programs. *Counselor Education & Supervision, 45*(3), 207–217.

෨ 5

THE DILEMMA OF PRACTICING AND TEACHING CONFIDENTIALITY WITHIN THE SCHOOL SETTING
Serving Multiple Agendas and Goals

Emily Phillips

Confidentiality as it relates to working with minors is the most challenging ethical dilemma educators face, especially for school counselors. "The assumption of confidentiality is a foundation for the counseling, consulting, assessment, transition and record-keeping functions. It is the foundation for the trust that helps individuals share intimate information with counselors truthfully."

—Baker & Gerler, 2004, p. 73

Chapter Overview

- Schools counselors' roles are radically different from those of mental health clinicians and educators in terms of stakeholders' input and guidelines/laws that must be considered.
- There is a lack of understanding regarding the roles school counselors play.
- Balancing the need to know against student/teacher/parent trust issues is challenging.
- Role conflict between consultant and counselor can affect ethical dilemmas of confidentiality.
- Teaching counselors-in-training about confidentiality is complex as there are few clear-cut answers and so many unique situations.

Inspirational Reflection

I began my career in a mental health clinic setting where the guidelines for confidentiality were very clear; there was to be no communication with school personnel or any other party without signed parental consent. Even with this consent, parents had to be very clear on what they wanted shared. Discussion with schools took place only when two-way releases by the parents were signed; these releases were infrequent, usually initiated by the school and were rather vague in terms of content offered and carefully worded. In fact, little was shared with the child's own parent(s) unless family sessions were held. The disadvantage, though, in working in the clinical setting was that almost all information came from a minor. Children's insight is usually limited and, owing to developmental level, cannot be regularly relied upon to be accurate. My personal shift from mental health work to the school setting was a challenge and brought with it more complex ethical dilemmas regarding confidentiality. It took me a few years to become comfortable sharing what I learned and to be better able to perform the necessary balancing act required in this role. I gradually came to respect the motivation behind teachers' requests and the need to involve them more in my work.

I found that in the educational setting I had frequent and easy access to other professionals and those invested in a child's life. It was a positive experience to share with others student concerns and successes. However, I quickly learned that with this increased access and contact, teachers, parents, principals, school psychologists, special education personnel, speech therapists, school nurses, bus drivers, and classroom aides wanted and expected information about children and their families. I also found that in this setting, the guidelines regarding confidentiality were more about ethics than laws. There are few laws to help guide confidentiality decisions in the school setting.

Laws and Ethics Relating to Confidentiality

The Family Educational Rights and Privacy Act, or the Buckley Amendment, passed in 1974, provides guidelines regarding the requirement for parental permission to release the records of minors. However, there are still many unclear areas in this law, including how school counselors keep and use their private notes and the sharing of information orally. The issue is further clouded by school counselors often being the only mental health professional in their building and maybe even in their district who has access to pertinent information that may help explain student distress. As a school counselor I was often privy to issues of anorexia, suicidal ideation, depression, child abuse, parental substance abuse, and other private issues that affected students' personal and academic success.

Counselors-in-training, as well as practicing school counselors, are bound by the Ethical Codes of the American Counseling Association (ACA, 2005), the American School Counseling Association (ASCA, 1998), and the Association for Specialists in Group Work (ASGW, 1998) at a minimum. In addition, in New York, where I work, we have a relatively new Ethical Code for Educators (New York State Education Department, 2002). Counselor educators are also bound by the ethical code of the Association for Counselor Education and Supervision (ACES).

Confidentiality Regarding Counseling

The National Standards for School Counseling Programs (Campbell & Dahir, 1997) and the National Model for School Counseling Programs (ASCA, 2004) emphasize that school counselors work with parents and teachers to address success in the areas of academic, career, and personal/social development. This uses the skills of counseling, consulting, guidance, curriculum, and coordination/collaboration. It is in the areas of counseling, collaboration, and consulting that the greatest dilemmas arise. Because school counselors work with minors, parents have the legal right to know what is going on in counseling. Technically, the rights of privacy belong to the parents, whether the student wishes this to be so or not. This creates another layer of ethical dilemma that needs to be addressed by practitioners.

As confidentiality is the cornerstone of a trusting counseling relationship, it is imperative that school counselors maintain the confidences of their students while simultaneously participating in educational team initiatives as consultants to better ensure student success and to eliminate barriers to learning. This team process can include multiple school personnel and parents as well as outside agencies and referral sources. Therefore, this confidentiality dilemma is a nearly constant struggle for school counselors and can create a dynamic tension within the educational environment, where the students' right to confidentiality needs to be weighed against others' need to know. This is rarely an easy decision, especially since teachers and school counselors often believe they do need to know in order to assist and support students better.

Confidentiality Regarding Consulting

The ACA Code of Ethics (2005) emphasizes the need to respect the privacy of clients. Yet, when clients are minors in the school setting, this respect can be difficult to maintain. School counselors are advised to have "minimal disclosure (Section B1F) except in those areas where the student is a danger, intends to endanger others or has committed an illegal act" (Section B1C). Even these areas can be interpreted in many ways and are not black and white. School counselors are told simultaneously that they are to "safeguard confidentiality" while simultaneously involving parents or guardians in the counseling process (Section B3).

The ASCA Ethical Standards (1998) are more school-oriented and suggest we inform students that it may be necessary to disclose some information when consulting with other professionals or if ordered to do so by a court. This code suggests that some private information may be shared in the school-based team process, yet also recommends that we remain consistent with our ethical obligations. This becomes quite a razor's edge. In addition, most school counselors also work with students in groups, and the Ethical Code for Group Counselors (1998) recommends that confidentiality in the group setting be expected, but acknowledges that it cannot be guaranteed.

Summary

It appears that although there are some professional resources to guide school counselors, whether they are in training or in practice, each individual counselor must judge the need to know against the consequences of breaching confidentiality and learn how to share necessary information without giving away highly personal details.

Counselor educators also struggle with the question of how to emphasize ethical responsibilities to counselors-in-training while simultaneously encouraging their roles as consultant and collaborator. These professors also have to highlight to those in training the need to please multiple stakeholders while simultaneously keeping the trust of their students.

Challenges Relating to Ethical Decision Making

There are legal, counseling, and consulting challenges that must be considered as part of ethical decision making for educators, especially for school counselors.

Laws and Ethical Challenges

One of the challenges relating to ethical decision making is that codes of ethics are living documents that change depending on the historical context. Therefore, school counselors must constantly remain connected to their professional organizations to be aware of these changes. For example, the latest ACA Code of Ethics has an expanded section on technology in counseling that includes both counseling as a service and the keeping of records and notes using technology. In addition, for counselor educators there is an expanded section on our responsibility as professors to recommend for the degree only those we believe will be successful. Temperamental and dispositional factors are always challenging to assess and even more so to use as criteria for eliminating students from degree programs. The ACES Code (1993) also guides us to not sponsor candidates who struggle with maintaining confidentiality.

In addition, since there are at least three codes of ethics relating to our parent professional organization, it can be complex and confusing to try to follow each without some conflict. In addition, there has been a dearth of literature on the topic of confidentiality, especially as it pertains to what is shared in team meetings. Few are researching and writing about this dilemma.

Counseling Challenges

In terms of individual dilemmas, it is extremely difficult with minors to decide what constitutes harm. The young may be so used to abuse that they underplay the harm being done to them. Furthermore, they may threaten suicide or to harm someone else when it may just be that they are letting off steam rather than that they have actual intent. It is difficult to know when to advise principals/parents and teachers on the need to monitor a student more closely. This is an even greater challenge when students return from treatment for things such as anorexia, alcoholism/substance abuse, or suicidal ideation. Although we certainly want to protect students from further harm, we as counselors cannot share such highly personal information with school personnel and may have expressly been told not to by a parent or guardian.

Consulting Challenges

In addition, school counselors are often privy to personal information shared by parents about themselves. It is extremely important that counselors respect the confidentiality of the adults' private business, such as the fact that they are struggling with alcoholism or that they are going through a divorce or facing domestic violence. Although certainly these issues may affect student behavior and performance, school counselors have to be very careful not to divulge this private information. If parents feel betrayed by the school counselor, they may deny counseling services for their child and undermine the treatment plan set up for the student in the classroom or with the team.

The younger the student, the more teachers and parents are needed to follow up on behavioral goals and to be part of the total treatment package to help ensure success. In fact, it is hard to change young students without the support and follow-through of families and teachers working on the same or similar goals. Vernon stated, "It is not a matter of whether to offer parent education and consultation but, rather, where, when, and in what format it should be provided" (2004, p. 428).

Also, historically, little to no clinical supervision is provided to practicing school counselors (Phillips, 2001) owing to the lack of similarly trained professionals in schools. Therefore, there are few who have a similar frame of reference and are bound by similar codes of ethics with whom school counselors can discuss these dilemmas.

Ethical Teaching Strategies

Practitioner Strategies

An important component of ethical practice is for school counselors to decide who the client is. Perhaps it is the parent who needs help with parenting strategies or a behavior modification plan. Maybe the client is the teacher who seems to struggle each year with "kids like that" (children who have ADHD, etc.). The dilemma of confidentiality for students might be eliminated if the "client" turns out not to be the student. So one key strategy is to determine whether the situation calls for counseling or consulting, which use similar skills but have different goals. Or perhaps a joint session can be scheduled with a student and a parent or teacher. This empowers children to discuss important issues for themselves and gives them life skills, rather than solving a single problem. It has been my professional experience—and Vernon (2004, p. 44) points out that many others who work with children agree—that often children want their parents and teachers to know about their discomfort and feelings so that change can occur, but that we may need to provide them with support, perhaps direct instruction in how to share their feelings, and help them choose what and how to tell.

Another strategy school counselors and teachers can use is to figure out the goals of information sharing. If the person seeking the information is simply curious, information can be shared at a minimal level. If the goal is to help a parent build a stronger bond with his/her child, then discussing strategies for accomplishing this and the child's feelings and reactions rather than specific details seems to circumvent the dilemma. If the goal is improved behavior in class, counselors and teachers working together to set up a contingency contract may be more helpful than knowledge of particular private details. In particular, school counselors need to be careful not to damage counseling relationships with children by relaying "venting" done by children regarding the adults in their lives. So working hard to determine whether the person seeking information has an "educational need to know" is essential (Salo & Shumante, 1993, p. 30). School counselors and teachers must regularly struggle to weigh the benefits against the possible harm to the student, parental, and counseling relationship. This is no easy task.

Certainly one thing counselors need to learn, and also help their staff learn, is how to determine true safety issues, such as danger to oneself or others, so that it becomes clearer when confidence must not be ensured and when it must be broken. They need to do this in a way that is least damaging to the relationships established. This can be done through regular and ongoing in-service dialogue with staff.

Teaching Strategies during Training

One teaching strategy that has helped me as a counselor educator is to teach counselors-in-training how to share information without breaking confidences. This is not easy to do. I provide multiple examples of how to develop a kind of "code" system with trusted teachers and other school personnel so they come to realize, through nuances of language and nonverbal cues, what the key issues are. I have trained students how to talk with parents so that they can focus on how the parent can help toward positive goals, without providing the exact information shared. I call this "talking around the issue, not about it." As a counselor educator I also talk with students about their need to keep private what teachers share with them about students and their families and to learn how to use this information in treatment and consultation without disclosing particulars or the source of the information. This can be a very challenging thing to do.

As educators we must teach the ethical codes, expect adherence to them, and also allow for discussion regarding the gray areas. One way I help with this is to include "critical incident" books in several of our graduate classes that allow students to deal vicariously with confidentiality and other ethical dilemmas. These books generally describe an incident and then have two expert opinions regarding how this could have been better handled and how the incident relates to various codes of ethics. These are available in counselor education through our professional association bookstore (ACA). Feedback from our students indicates that they find these books very helpful in directing them to think through situations before they are placed in them. The emphasis in training is placed on being intentional and reflective regarding therapeutic issues before disclosing and considering carefully what students wish or what needs they are trying to meet through their disclosure. In teacher preparation programs similar casebooks and critical incident books can provide safe, guided practice on ethical dilemmas. Teacher candidates would benefit from some exposure to the roles and ethical codes of school counselors since they will work so closely together in the school. It would be helpful if school administration programs also provided this exposure.

More states developing codes of ethics for educators similar to New York's would help make educators aware of, and increase their thinking about, the consequences of breaking confidentiality. For example, the New York State Code, Principle 5, states that "[e]ducators respect the private nature of the special knowledge they have about students and their families and use that knowledge only in the students' best interests" (New York State Education Department, 2002, para 6).

Time must be allotted in class during training for all educators for discussion on conflicts that are likely to arise. This is particularly true of fieldwork courses where candidates are beginning their practice. Close supervision by the on-site and campus-based supervisors is needed as students might not even be aware that they are involved in a confidentiality issue. My students are often shocked at what is discussed in faculty lounges at schools and the "scuttlebutt" shared at team meetings. The professor can address these issues each semester, even if students do not bring them up.

In addition, most counseling programs have students sign ethical pledges of confidentiality in classes where sharing of a more personal nature is likely or encouraged to occur and also when doing their field experiences. We emphasize the negative consequences of idle disclosure on clients and colleagues-in-training, and that failure to follow these directives can result not only in client harm but also in dismissal from our program.

Finally, we need to encourage our graduates to join their professional organizations, to stay current on their codes of ethics, and to join listservs and other networking opportunities at the local, regional, state, and national levels so that they can participate in ongoing dialogue on these topics.

Synthesis of Ethical Lessons Learned

In summary, one of the most frustrating issues is that the answer to the topic of confidentiality as an ethical dilemma in a school-based setting is rarely black or white. There are so many shades of gray, and each parent, student, teacher, principal, and situation must be handled uniquely.

Counselors and teachers need to learn whom they can trust, and they need to expect to get burned at times. This can be a painful lesson, especially if there is damage to a student or parent relationship if confidentiality is breached.

The responsibility falls on the counselor to train the staff and even the parents on what their role is and to share with others that they are bound by codes of ethics, what the consequences of breaching confidentiality could be, and how to best use school counselors as a resource. This needs to be done with tact and diplomacy so that school counselors do not come across as not being team players or as not wanting to help. It is up to the counselors to help other educators understand and respect their role, and they must also respect the information shared with them by others.

Educators need to learn, and to help others with whom they consult, to focus on solutions rather than on obtaining specific information. And, finally, more research needs to be done in this area for both counselors and teachers so that both training institutions and practitioners can continue to address this complex topic.

Questions for Consideration

Consider the consequences of venting in the faculty room after an upsetting child abuse case or a frustrating parent meeting.

Reflect on what a parent might do if private information shared with you has gotten back to him/her. How might this impact his/her relationship with you and the school counselor's work with that child?

Supplementary Resources

Guided Practice with Ethical Dilemmas: Herlihy, B., & Corey, G. (Eds.). *ACA ethical standards casebook* (6th ed.). Alexandria, VA: American Counseling Association. This book discusses typical ethical dilemmas counselors might face.

Exemplary Critical Incidents and Strategies: Tyson, L., & Pedersen, P. (2000). *Critical incidents in school counseling.* Alexandria, VA: American Counseling Association. This book provides specific school-based ethical dilemmas that are responded to by two "expert opinions."

Reflective Professional Development: Schön, D. A. (1983). *The reflective practitioner: How professionals think in action.* Cambridge, MA: Basic Books. This resource covers not just the field of education but many professional trainings and asks us to consider how we focus too much on theoretical and scientific knowledge and rarely stop to reflect. We are often reactors rather than reflectors. The author also does an excellent job of describing the developmental process that novices go through from first being able to reflect retrospectively (looking back after the fact) to being able to reflect in the moment and adapt strategies.

Kottler, J. (1993). *On becoming a teacher: The human dimension.* Thousand Oaks, CA: Corwin Press. This resource helps educators-in-training consider the personal dimensions of teaching and education and promotes taking a whole-child approach to education. Although an older book, it is a seminal work in the field.

Kottler, J. (2005). *The emerging professional counselor: Student dreams to professional realities.* Alexandria, VA: American Counseling Association. This resource helps both novices and counselors think about their ethical decision making and to consider the psychological shifts that need to be made to become a professional.

Schön, D. A. (1986). *Educating the reflective practitioner: Toward a new design for teaching and learning in the professions.* San Francisco, CA: Jossey-Bass. This resource looks at the job of educators at the university level and assists them to consider how to include reflective practice into their course design.

References

American Counseling Association. (2005). *ACA code of ethics.* Alexandria, VA: Author.

American School Counseling Association. (1998). *ASCA code of ethics for school counselors.* Alexandria, VA: Author.

————. (2004). *The ASCA national model.* Alexandria, VA: Author.

Association for Counselor Education and Supervision. (1993). *Ethical code for counselor educators and supervisors.* Alexandria, VA: Author.

Association for Specialists in Group Work. (1998). *Ethical code of the Association for Specialists in Group Work.* Alexandria, VA: Author.

Baker, S., & Gerler, E. (2004). *School counseling for the 21st century* (4th ed.). Upper Saddle River, NJ: Pearson.

Campbell, C., & Dahir, C. (1997). *The national standards for school counseling programs.* Alexandria, VA: American Counseling Association.

New York State Education Department. (2002). *Ethical code for educators.* Retrieved April, 1, 2007, from www.highered.nysed.gov/tcert/resteachers/codeofethics.htm#statement.

Phillips, E. (2001). First assignment elementary school counselors' perceived needs for supervision. *The Journal for the Professional Counselor, (16)*2, 51–65.

Salo, M., & Shumante, S. (1993). In T. Remley (Ed.), *The ACA legal series: Counseling minor clients.* Volume 4. Alexandria, VA: American Counseling Association.

Vernon, A. (2004). *Counseling children and adolescents* (3rd ed.). Denver, CO: Love Publishing.

ETHICAL RESISTANCE IN TEACHER EDUCATION
Calling Out the Truth Telling in Academia

Jennifer Goeke and Deborah Eldridge

Chapter Overview

- An educator's experience of resisting the dominant discourse in teacher education.
- Examining the space for multiple perspectives on teaching in teacher education.
- Strategies for challenging the pseudocommunity in academia.

Throughout this chapter there are two voices, I and we. The "I" voice represents the individual experience of the first author, Jennifer. The "we" voice represents shared experiences or viewpoints. Both authors, Jennifer and Deb, strongly believe that the silencing of "I" experiences in teacher education should be resisted. "I" and "we" can become "us" if truthtelling and calling each other out on popularized viewpoints becomes the accepted practice of scholars who actively seek to transform themselves into a real, not psuedo, community.

Inspirational Reflection

I have been called a *behaviorist*. Over the course of my first four years in academia, my colleagues in teacher education—some of whom are award-winning scholars and widely acknowledged geniuses—have (a) asked me whether I kept my infant son in a Skinner box; (b) called me atheoretical; and (c) insinuated that my doctoral education must have been considerably subpar. When I told a colleague I had been offered a contract to write a book on direct instruction, there was silence, followed by, "What made you write *that*?" Just yesterday a new colleague turned to me and said, "Can you believe that a student in my class actually said that behaviorism is a valid teaching methodology?" I looked at her and replied, "It *is* a valid teaching methodology." She sat quietly for a moment, looked at me in horror, and uttered, "B-b-but, you're not a behaviorist, *are you*?"

The funny thing is that I am not now, nor have I ever been, a behaviorist. From a theoretical standpoint, I actually consider myself to be a systems person (I even included a reading by Salvador Minuchin in my wedding ceremony). When you are used to viewing the world through a systems lens, you see imbalances and you try to figure out ways to put things back in balance. Among my peers I seem to be virtually alone in insisting that we retain balance as we reconceptualize learning and teaching for our increasingly diverse schools. If there are others who share my view, they are not revealing themselves and I cannot say I blame them.

I arrived at this perspective the hard way, as a beginning teacher in a second-grade inclusive classroom. Robert was a student in my first second-grade class. His mother brought him to meet me one day as I was excitedly preparing my classroom. She sheepishly introduced him: "This is Robert. He can't read." I assured Robert's mother that my approach to teaching would get Robert reading. He probably lacked confidence and needed a caring teacher who could change his attitude toward reading. I was more than prepared to deal with Robert's difficulties. In my class, reading would be fun!

As the year progressed, Robert's attitude toward reading did not change. In fact, it got worse. It got so bad by the spring of that year that Robert went from an introverted, sullen boy to a full-fledged behavior problem. One day, after I had repeatedly asked him to take out a book and begin reading, he took off his shoes, tied them together, and threw them at me, yelling, "I-CAN'T-READ!" I can still hear his angry enunciation of the words. It literally took Robert to hit me over the head with his shoes for me to realize that he did not need me to change his attitude or boost his confidence; he needed me to teach him *how to read*. I am embarrassed, in retrospect, by my willful naïveté. I persisted in my belief that I was doing the best for my students long past the point when I should have realized that in neglecting their instructional needs, I was actually doing them harm. Robert would go to third grade having neither acquired nor mastered a single reading skill in my classroom. I felt that I had worked so hard. I had exhausted myself, staying in my classroom for hours after school devising creative learning activities and designing a rich literacy environment. I tirelessly performed everything my teacher preparation had taught me was not only effective but *right*, and yet I had failed—miserably.

My devastating experience with Robert (and several others like him) led me to a critical reconsideration of my approach to teaching. During the next few years, I doggedly pursued every professional development avenue to remake myself into an expert—and truly inclusive—teacher. Along the way, I met many other teachers with similar experiences. I discovered that my teacher education had developed only one extreme end of a full continuum of essential teaching skills and strategies. With time and reflection, I became embittered by what I felt was the willful and purposeful exclusion by my professors of knowledge that they probably knew I would need but preferred not to teach.

Challenges Relating to Ethical Truth-Telling

All of this happened in 1994, so you'll understand why I might be shocked by the fact that twelve years later, I still see imbalance and irrationality in teacher education. Only now, I get to view it up close because to my occasional dismay, I'm one of them. I have smart colleagues who are deeply committed to democracy in education, particularly for diverse students. In my school of education, we have a mission statement, a portrait of an ideal teacher, and many other documents where democratic principles are strongly—almost cultishly— explicated. But for me, the way we throw around the word democracy is starting to give it the same empty ring it has when politicians use it. What I cannot understand is why people who are so committed to diversity would declare that a single form of teaching (i.e., constructivism) is best for millions of students in schools—students who do not share the same skills, motivation, fluency in English, prior knowledge, or experience.

Herein lies an ethical challenge to telling the truth about our beliefs and ideas in teacher education in general: How do we stay professionally "open" and expressive about our diverse directions, perspectives, and approaches on the basis of personal experiences and beliefs? And how do we allow our differing perspectives to live together and enrich each other, or don't we?

I became a professor because I believed that voices like mine—committed to rational, effective inclusive education—would find a place. Sadly, I have struggled to find my place or, more specifically, my "people." I do not exactly fit in with my colleagues in general education, for reasons described above. And although my colleagues in special education say, "Why do you concern yourself with those people? Just hang with us!," I do not fit neatly into their world either. I believe in the value of the full continuum of teaching methods, from the most structured of behaviorist approaches to the most student-centered of constructivist ones. A teacher who can assess students' learning needs and masterfully apply the most effective method for them at that moment, for that particular skill, strategy, content, or concept, just seems better to me than a teacher who rigidly adheres to his or her own preferred model. After all, as I learned, it is not about what *you* believe to be right, it is about what is right for your students.

It is only natural that as a systems person, I have thought a lot about how the imbalance in my teacher preparation has replicated itself in my career as a teacher educator. The real world of schools has been growing increasingly diverse and inclusive since before I became a classroom teacher. Yet faculty—and, as a result, students—in teacher preparation programs continue to have two very distinct and conflicting views of educators. General educators are viewed as masters of the art of teaching, whereas special educators are masters of the science. General educators focus on big ideas such as caring, democratic, child-centered practice, whereas special educators promote practices such as differentiated instruction, universal design for learning, and functional behavioral assessment. Let's face it, big ideas are seductive because they just sound better. In our current culture, some people even give war a pass if it is done in the name of democracy. Conversely, when my colleagues hear that I think behaviorism has its place, they assume by extension that I must not be very caring or democratic or child-centered; nothing could be further from the truth. When they assume that my doctoral training was simplistic, they apply the same reductionism to my expertise that is often applied to the curriculum and expectations for students with disabilities. Is it any wonder that general and special educators in the field struggle to collaborate effectively? They are acting out our dysfunction.

Many of my colleagues in teacher education appear to retain a politics of difference that pathologizes or exoticizes the Other, even as they vociferously advocate democracy and diversity. Said differently, they continue to buy into difference as impairment, but only when it comes to disabilities. Faculty with expertise considered different and separate from the "normal" curriculum are excluded, not by location but by the discourses that dominate our encounters. We need teacher educators who can see beyond antiquated, bifurcated, and elitist notions of expertise and reconceptualize inclusive teaching as a cohesive blend of science *and* art—and as positive, normal, and desirable.

The binaries that divide me from my general education colleagues are not just theoretical; they are also pedagogical. It is widely held that if we immerse teacher education students in dispositions (through discussion, reflection, journaling, case analyses, and other constructivist methods), they'll go out into the field and teach themselves what they need to know about instruction. There are several things that disturb me about this line of thinking. First, teachers—especially those in our nation's highly segregated schools—need to hit the ground running. You cannot teach yourself anything when the day-to-day reality of your job is physically, emotionally, and intellectually exhausting.

Second, it perpetuates the impression of teacher educators as "meaning makers" who do not actually care about preparing effective teachers. It exposes us to criticism from those outside education who can smell our arrogance, and it is doing the direct opposite of *caring* about our own students in teacher education. What caring teacher would instructionally disable her students and then send them into one of the most demanding situations they could ever face?

Ethical Calling-Out Strategies

There are buzzwords in teacher education that we all mouth: social justice, democratic practices, appreciation for diversity, knowledge construction, and on and on. However, the more we mouth them, the more we fail to examine them critically. The more we mouth them, the more we diminish the alternatives and differences in perspectives that academia purports to embrace. The more we mouth them, the more we become a *pseudocommunity* that plays at being a community by acting as if we all agree (Grossman, Wineburg, & Woolworth, 2001). A pseudocommunity is one in which "there is no authentic sense of shared communal space but only individuals interacting with other individuals" (p. 956). The heart of ethical resistance in teacher education means calling out the acts that sustain psuedocommunity and employing strategies for the creation of a real community of scholars.

The first strategy is to find the time to get to know one another as "thinkers and learners" (p. 953). Creating opportunities to talk about our work as scholars is a luxury in teacher education. Approaching such opportunities with an open, *receiving* posture requires time; it is hard to sandwich conversation and discovery among the classes we teach, the papers we write, and the meetings we attend. Often, talking together with the intention of getting to know each other as thinkers and learners seems like too much of a luxury and too little related to tenure and promotion. *But,* we make the time for what we value most. If we do not start to value what sustains and nurtures us as colleagues and scholars, then we deserve what we get: a pseudocommunity that *acts* as if everyone agrees.

A second strategy for ethical resistance to perpetuating a pseudocommunity is to agree to "navigate the fault lines" (p. 989). This means to accept that there are and will be disagreements, to welcome these conflicts as opportunities to sort out what we mean and what we believe, and to broaden our capacity to agree to disagree. We need not, as academics, believe that intellectual harmony is our ultimate goal. Our professional goal must be to speak the truth as we see it to each other and to stand unafraid in the face of counterevidence. With this strategy we do not seek to dilute each other's beliefs or arrive at a common (and false) consensus. On the contrary, by navigating the fault lines we honor each other and ourselves with the depth and breadth of our perspectives.

Although there may be others, we conclude with a third recommendation that is more a commitment than a strategy per se. An indicator of a professional community "is the willingness of its members to assume responsibility for colleagues' growth and development" (p. 989). Responsibility for a colleague's growth and development does not mean pressing your point of view until your colleague adopts it or is subsumed by it. True communities of practice are informed by caring relationships and marked by responsiveness, reciprocity, and dialogue (Noddings, 1992). We acknowledge that caring for each other's work and ideas involves questioning and sharing in an attempt to understand, not persuade, each other. We welcome, even encourage, each other to speak out, to call each other out, and to tell the truth as we know it. We talk and question in order to learn. We resist, ethically, in order to grow.

Synthesis of Ethical Lessons Learned

For me, the overarching lesson of my experience as a teacher and as a teacher educator is that we cannot continue to conceptualize teaching as an enterprise devoted to the *normal* students in our classrooms and expect teachers to figure out how to tack on an accommodation for the exceptions. Rather, we must attend to the creation of a positive pedagogy that centers rather than marginalizes diversity—broadly defined to include all diversity, including disability. In addressing these concerns, it is essential to acknowledge that students with disabilities are not the only ones who will benefit from this positive pedagogy. Intensive and sustained effort toward the acceptance and improvement of inclusive teaching is the path toward true social justice for all students.

As teacher educators, we need to apply this lesson to ourselves and become less superficially and more honestly committed to a diverse range of professional outcomes: the need to promote caring, democracy, and social justice as well as to rethink and problematize the simplistic binaries that divide us (constructivism–behaviorism; art–science; normal–abnormal; general ed–special ed; diversity narrowly defined–diversity broadly defined). The question is not whether we perceive differences among ourselves but, rather, the meaning that we bring to bear on our perceived differences. We must challenge one another to be as progressive as our rhetoric suggests we are and start modeling the kind of collaboration and inclusive practice that we expect of our students. If the consensus is that we have only so much time and we cannot do it all, then we need to conduct research together that finds better, more efficient, and more effective ways of doing it.

Questions for Consideration

In a faculty meeting a colleague states, "We should all be teaching about social justice in our classes." What do you think your colleague means? Is your view a shared one? How do you know? What do you do? Agree? Stay silent?

You plan a classroom activity around a video. Two of your students take a stand against it by questioning you critically about your rationale for choosing it and their need to watch it. How do you respond? Be honest. How would you feel and what would you do under these circumstances?

You have been asked to join two colleagues in writing a curriculum for your school. Your perspectives on what needs to be in the curriculum are divergent. How do you proceed? Do you drop out and let them go it alone? Do you re-solve to contribute and try to change their minds?

Supplementary Resources

Build Your Ethical-Dilemma-Responding Muscles: Check out the Web site of the Institute for Global Ethics at http://www.globalethics.org/resources/dilemmas.htm. It has real-life ethical dilemmas contributed by the institute's membership in the areas of education and child/family life, among others. The site offers a featured dilemma such as the following, downloaded on February 9, 2007:

Good Coach, But Bad Role Model
Jim is a basketball coach with more than two decades of experience; he has coached his teams through several national championships, winning two of them. But there have been many alleged reports of vulgar incidents and violent and abusive behavior towards team members over the years.

Character Challenge Site for Students: Another Web site of interest is the goodcharacter.com site at http://www.goodcharacter.com/dilemma/dilemma.html. The site presents ethical dilemmas for discussion with students. There are currently sixteen scenarios and discussion questions for teachers to use with their students. The site also has a feature for you to share the results of your discussions.

References

Grossman, P., Wineburg, S., & Woolworth, S. (2001). Toward a theory of teacher community. *Teachers College Record, 103*(6), 942–1012.

Noddings, N. (1992). *The challenge to care in schools: An alternative approach to education.* New York: Teachers College Press.

ℭℜ 7

NUTS AND BOLTS
Federal Regulations and Local Institutional Review Boards

Joye Smith

[These] principles, respect for persons, beneficence, and justice, are now accepted as the three quintessential requirements for the ethical conduct of research involving human subjects.

— *Introduction, Institutional Review Board Guidebook*

Chapter Overview

- How do the federal regulations for research using human subjects apply to educational research?
- What are institutional review boards, and what are the procedures for submitting a research proposal for their review?
- What special regulations are in effect for university student research and research in school settings?

Inspirational Reflection

My reflections on institutional review boards (IRBs) and their role in safeguarding the rights of research participants began on a positive note during my doctoral research. I loved research, loved the conception of a project, the thinking through of the procedures, but I had never had any systematic instruction in the protection of human subjects. When I sought permission from the institution to do my research, the IRB responded and asked me to submit a proposal. Up to that point, I had never even heard of IRBs, and the thought of allowing them to see my work was intimidating. Frankly, I was concerned that I would not be able to give them what they wanted and would be prevented from continuing. Researching my own interests seemed pristine and elegant and solitary; to invite an outside party to review it somehow muddied the waters, inviting scrutiny and, yes, potential rejection.

Fortunately, my fears, at least on this occasion, were unfounded. This IRB was reasonable: they set certain boundaries on my data collection, to avoid the perception of coercion, but they were, overall, very supportive of my research. They explained, in a respectful and transparent way, why they were asking for certain things, and I began to learn about some of their concerns. This positive experience extended to my full-time faculty position in a college where, owing to an extensive faculty education program and a level-headed chairperson, the IRB had a good working relationship with most researchers.

However, I soon discovered that not all IRBs are supportive or reasonable. Because I am on the education faculty of a college, I am expected (and want) to do research in our partner schools. I submitted a proposal to the IRB of our local school board to do some simple, low-risk observational research to supplement quantitative data collection. In response, they made demands that were impossible for me to meet, and the research could not be performed. My reflections on IRBs at this point were not very positive. I was frustrated about the study, and I felt my integrity was being questioned.

Finally, I was asked to be part of our college's IRB and so began a new phase of reflection on issues of academic freedom, faculty research, publication and tenure, the potential for litigation, and safety and privacy. Now that I am on the other side of proposal review, I experience much more keenly the tension between the freedom to do research and the need to protect subjects. On the one hand, many of my negative feelings toward IRBs have evaporated. I have begun to appreciate the difficult mission that has been given to IRBs and the added challenges they face in a society that is increasingly fragmented, litigious, and predatory. Before, I would probably have agreed with Gordon (2003) that IRBs' hypervigilance is more often about protecting the institution against litigation than it is about protecting human subjects. Now that I have seen dozens of research proposals and the (thankfully) rare case that seriously threatens safety and privacy, I find the threat of litigation to be minor in comparison. Some of what I have seen done in the name of research would make anyone hypervigilant about the protection of human subjects. On the other hand, I am also a faculty researcher. This makes me especially sensitive to the most serious faculty complaint, that the IRB review process slows down or even impedes the progress of faculty research.

Since I have begun to live in this tension and wrestle with its implications, I have reflected on what causes it, what makes it, at times, so rancorous, and what can be done to remedy it. It is true that there are "problem IRBs." There are those that do not function at all, and then there are what Pritchard (2002) calls the IRB "trolls" (p. 3), intent on charging ridiculous tolls and generally making it difficult to cross the bridge. These are the IRBs that never give permission until after at least five or six revisions of the proposal, if then.

However, even with a healthy, functioning IRB making reasonable requests, the faculty response can be one of frustration and belligerence, if not outright hostility. I know that it is not that my colleagues wish harm to their subjects. Rather, in many cases, I think it is the very distinctive language of the IRB, taken from the federal regulations, that may cause misunderstanding and raise defenses. More than an ideological divide, it is as if the IRB and the researcher were speaking two mutually incomprehensible languages. An illustration of this in print is the exchange between Levine (1983) and the chair of the IRB that reviewed his study (Lathrop, 1983). The dispute seemed to center around their understanding of the concept of risk. Levine (1983) had wanted to interview hospital employees about "their experience with court-ordered institutional change" (p. 8). He took a common sense view of risk, claiming that the publication of his study in "an obscure scholarly monograph" posed less potential harm than, say, an interview for a newspaper (p. 9). The hospital IRB, however, viewed the potential risk to the employees' confidentiality as a central issue, particularly since the topic of their interviews was still in active litigation. The IRB's requests for clarification, which seemed to Levine to be bureaucratic obstruction, were, in their minds, necessary to determine whether the study's benefits outweighed the risks. Here we have two entirely different interpretations of the same incident, a situation that I believe was due, in some measure, to the language used in the correspondence.

How is this tension to be resolved? In my own journey, the first steps included learning the language of the IRB and becoming open to seeing my research from an entirely new perspective. In the process of reading about the history of human subjects' protections, I discovered that I shared the values on which the IRB's mission rests. I also recognized, through the ups and downs of my own proposal reviews, that the world is becoming more interconnected. For a solitary professor to do research in an ivory tower is no longer possible, if ever it was. With greater interconnection comes the demand for greater accountability. As a part of this accountability, the IRB review is an important safeguard for researchers. It warns them against being more concerned with attaining their research goals, publishing their findings, getting tenure and promotion, and earning a wider reputation than with protecting those who are involved in their study. The IRB review can provide a powerful reminder to educational researchers that their research subjects are not just means to an end. They are (or are represented by) autonomous moral agents "whose interests must be acknowledged even though their interests may be unrelated to or threatened by the interest of the research activity" (Pritchard, 2002, p. 4). They are to be regarded "not only as objects, but as subjects" (p. 4).

When we complain that IRBs are too biomedically oriented or do not understand research approaches used by the educational community, let us not forget the scores of untested, dull, counterproductive, or even dangerous educational experiments that have been performed on unsuspecting minors and adults over the years, without informed consent and without any hint that the approaches were effective at anything but maintaining someone's idea of the status quo. It is easy to criticize those who took Native American children from their homes and forced them to learn in English only or those who made left-handed children write with their right hand (Anderson & Arsenaut, 1998), but it is much harder to be aware of our own blind spots. Learning the history of human subjects' protection, the origins of the legal language, and the procedures for meeting the demands of one's local IRB will, I hope, be a step in the direction of mutual understanding, self-understanding, and growth.

Challenges Related to Ethical Decision Making

In recent years, academic journals have begun requiring authors whose research involves human beings to submit an approval letter from an IRB along with their articles. In many college settings, IRB approval is now required for master's theses as well as doctoral dissertations that involve the study of human subjects. As an IRB member at my college, as well as an education faculty member, I experience the tension between faculty, who need the freedom to explore their field of inquiry, and the IRB, which must ensure that human subjects are being treated fairly, humanely, and justly. My purpose in this chapter is to answer some basic questions about the IRB so that educators and their students can be better prepared to meet its demands and to streamline the process of getting approval to use human subjects. What are IRBs and what is their purpose? How do the federal regulations for research using human subjects apply in education settings? What does one need to do to submit an IRB proposal? What about research performed by graduate students and research in schools with minors?

Origins of Ethical Research

Systematic descriptions of ethical treatment of research subjects have their origin largely in medical practice and ethics, both ancient and modern. Physicians throughout ancient history were exhorted, for example, to maintain their patients' confidentiality (Veatch & Mason, 1987). These ethics are surprisingly similar across cultures and over time. Tsai (1999) reports that the ethical principles followed by modern Western biomedical researchers are largely, if not completely, reflected in the ethics of ancient Chinese medicine. Unfortunately, ethical standards have often been applied in a discriminatory fashion. Washington describes a number of injustices committed against people of color over the past two centuries in her recent book *Medical Apartheid* (2006), but she sets them against the commonly accepted ethics of the time for the treatment (of whites) in hospitals, medical schools, and other institutions (p. 73). In modern times, regulations protecting all human subjects regardless of ethnic background originated in a set of directives known as the Nuremberg Code (1949), developed for the Nuremberg Military Tribunal to use as it scrutinized the so-called medical research of the Nazi regime. The code enumerated a number of principles that have become central to our understanding of human subjects' protection, most notably that of voluntary and informed consent. Subjects must be legally able to give consent, must not be subject to coercion, and must understand enough of the study to be able to make an informed and voluntary judgment about participation.

In 1974, subsequent to revelations about such studies as the Tuskegee Experiment (Jones, 1993), the U.S. government created the first regulations protecting human subjects and established IRBs as one mechanism to ensure that protection. A commission was appointed at the same time to recommend the basic ethical principles that should underlie all biomedical and behavioral research. Their findings were presented in what became known as the Belmont Report (1979). The three guiding principles of the Belmont Report are as follows: (1) respect for persons, which is tied to informed, voluntary consent, including the right of subjects to withdraw from the study at any time and not participate in any part of the study if they choose (e.g., not being obliged to answer every question on a survey); (2) beneficence, which takes into consideration the probabilities and extent of potential risks and benefits, and the minimization of risk; and (3) justice, which mandates fair selection criteria and not selection merely because subjects are vulnerable and cannot say "no."

Because so much of the language of the federal regulations on research using human subjects has evolved from concerns about biomedical research, school teachers and college professors may ask themselves whether it is appropriate to consider behavioral research in general, and educational research in particular, through the same lens. However, any research, given the right circumstances, can be risky for the subjects, can put their privacy and reputation at risk, or can subject them to physical danger or emotional distress. These factors are what IRBs examine when they review any study, regardless of the field of inquiry. In some ways, in fact, behavioral research can be riskier than some biomedical research because it involves unpredictable human responses.

Consider a study on battered women or abused children and the additional risks that they would be subjected to if their identities were made known or the nature of the study was revealed to their abusers. Even in educational research, a seemingly innocent question about "feeling blue" on a survey given to adolescents might have unintended consequences that the researcher and the IRB must anticipate. A study in a school that includes the use of, say, photos of children at work in the classroom needs to include assurances that the photos, which can potentially be used to identify specific children, have been obtained with parental permission and are safely secured from unintended disclosure to third parties.

Most researchers assess the benefits and risks of their study fairly and objectively; however, even conscientious investigators may place subjects at risk without realizing it. If, for example, they were to attempt to recruit parents of HIV-infected children directly before the parents had agreed to be involved in the study (say, by responding to posted flyers), the investigators may inadvertently reveal the children's HIV status to third parties and place the subjects' reputations and privacy at risk. The IRB review can catch potential risks or problems that the researcher may have missed, making the study better and safer.

The Institutional Review Board

Institutional Review Boards are the local bodies that apply the federal regulations of the Office of Human Research Protections (OHRP), located in the Department of Health and Human Services (HHS). The HHS regulations, derived from the Belmont Report and codified in Title 45 Code of Federal Regulations Part 46 (2005; hereafter 45 CFR 46), help to guide an IRB's decision whether to approve proposed research using human subjects. The CFR defines a human subject as "a living individual about whom an investigator (whether professional or student) conducting research obtains (1) Data through intervention or interaction with the individual, or (2) Identifiable private information" (45 CFR 46.102(f), 2001).

If the IRB's main job is to review proposed research in terms of the treatment of human subjects, then what is research? The Code of Federal Regulations defines it in this way:

> [Research is] a systematic investigation, including research development, testing and evaluation, designed to develop or contribute to *generalizable knowledge*. Activities which meet this definition constitute research for purposes of this policy, whether or not they are conducted or supported under a program which is considered research for other purposes. For example, some demonstration and service programs may include research activities. (45 CFR 46.102(d), 2001; italics added)

It is possible that certain activities labeled "research" may not be intended to contribute to generalizable knowledge, whereas others not labeled as such may, in fact, be research. Thus, work compiling facts and artifacts in order to write a history of the education of immigrants in New Jersey in the late nineteenth century may be called research by the author. However, if the book does not intend to contribute to generalizable knowledge about immigration patterns, responses by the educational community to immigration, and so on, then it is not considered research according to the federal regulations.

There are three categories of research described by the federal code, determined by the level of risk for subjects. First, there are "exempt" studies (see Appendix A, p. 76). The term is unfortunate, because even though the federal regulations do not require such studies to be reviewed by an IRB, most IRBs are required by their institutions to review every study for which they are responsible, even exempt, low-risk, educational research. Exempt for most IRBs, then, would mean "exempt from continuing review," that is, reviewed only once. Exempt studies include research into "normal educational practices" and using "test results that do not reveal personal identifiers." An example of a study of "normal educational practices" would be the teacher who is testing a new type of calculator or a new curriculum approach in one of her mathematics classes to see the impact on student learning. Also, studies that use test results without personal identifiers such as name, social security number, and date of birth are considered exempt because they cannot be traced back to individual test-takers.

The second category is called "expedited." Expedited studies are approved for no more than one year at a time and are riskier than exempt studies, requiring a consent form in most cases. Investigators must reapply for approval each year, reporting adverse events or subjects withdrawing from the study. A list of the types of expedited studies can be found in Appendix B (p. 77). The most pertinent for educators are (5) using existing data that was collected for non-research purposes; (6) voice, video, digital, or image recordings of human behavior; and (7) research on individual or group characteristics or behavior data collected through survey, interview, oral history, or focus groups, for example, where subjects can be identified. An example of an expedited study includes a researcher convening and then audiotaping a focus group of teachers discussing the effectiveness of different approaches to professional development. The teachers' identities are known to the researcher and to one another and may be surmised from the audiotape by a third party, even if the researcher uses pseudonyms in her transcriptions and final report. A consent form is required from the teachers, and the researcher must take special care to store the tape and transcripts securely.

Full committee studies are those being considered for federal funding, are riskier or more complex, perhaps multi-site, studies, or are studies that have been found to be problematic and that require discussion by the entire, convened committee. They can be approved for no more than one year at a time, similar to expedited studies. Large-scale literacy projects that are gathering data in several local school districts, for example, would probably require full committee review because of the complexity of the documentation required.

The best advice I can give when dealing with an IRB is not to make assumptions; ask about its policies so that you can make informed decisions and save yourself time and trouble. One researcher contacted us to say that he was writing a history of some neighborhoods in the city in which we live. He wondered whether he needed to submit an IRB proposal. Even though we suspected that his work was intended as particular knowledge about historical events rather than generalizable knowledge, we asked him to submit a proposal. It is important for us to see what the researcher is actually planning to do, what his or her objectives are, and what procedures are intended for data collection, to make that determination. He graciously met our request, and we quickly concluded that it was indeed not research according to the federal guidelines. We only asked that he contact us if the focus of his inquiry changed. Even though his study was not subject to IRB review, he understood that he was responsible, as are all investigators, for conducting his work in an ethical manner.

Procedures

There are three steps to submitting an IRB proposal. First, the researcher (also called the principal investigator or PI) and any research assistants involved must complete a training session in research using human subjects. One user-friendly online version used by a number of institutions is the Collaborative IRB Training Initiative's (CITI) Course in the Protection of Human Research Subjects (www.citiprogram.org). It consists of a series of modules on different aspects of ethical treatment of human subjects. Each module contains a reading on that topic, followed by test questions. The training does not have to be completed at one sitting, and there are different levels of exam training, depending on whether the researcher is a student, an instructor, or an IRB member. The tutorial is so thorough and accessible that we have incorporated it as a requirement in some of our graduate research courses.

Second, the researcher will describe the research in a proposal to the IRB and complete an IRB application (either on paper or online), keeping in mind that she or he may be addressing IRB members who are not experts in that field. Our IRB encourages the PI to include the following eight items in his or her description of the research, on the basis of the federal regulations (45 CFR 46.111, 2001); your IRB may have a slightly different set of questions.

1. The purpose of the research, its major hypotheses and research design (or research questions and grounded research context if it is qualitative or ethnographic). We encourage researchers to include relevant background research for non-expert readers.

2. The source of subjects and selection criteria (providing advertisements and flyers, if used).

3. Description of procedures with enough detail so that we can easily visualize what subjects would be asked to do and how the PI would interact with subjects (providing copies of questionnaires, interview schedules, tests, etc.).

4. Description of potential risks and benefits.

5. Description of how confidentiality and anonymity will be protected, including data coding systems, how and where data will be stored, who will have access to them, and what will happen to them after the study is completed.

6. Description of debriefing process if "deception" has occurred, and what the PI would do if a medical or other potentially troubling condition occurred. Deception refers to incomplete disclosure of the exact nature of the research to subjects prior to the study, to avoid an expectancy bias. Deception may only be used if the study cannot reasonably proceed without it and if subjects are fully informed about the nature of the study when it is done (Department of Health and Human Services, [b]).

7. Description of consent processes (attach consent forms and translations, if needed).

8. Any other pertinent information that might be relevant to the IRB's decision.

(Taken from "Application for Approval," n.d.)

Third, once the proposal has been submitted, the review process begins. Exempt and expedited studies can be reviewed by individual members of the IRB committee as they come in. In the individual reviews, IRB members exercise all of the committee's authority, including approving low-risk studies, except that they cannot reject a study (45 CFR 46.110(b)(2), 2001). Instead, if they have serious concerns, they can bring the study to a full committee meeting. The convened IRB committee may accept the study, ask questions for clarification, ask for revisions, or reject the study outright. The PI cannot recruit subjects, distribute consent or information forms, or begin to collect data until the IRB approves the study.

Recruiting subjects and obtaining consent. Subjects must be given the opportunity to learn about the nature of the study and to freely and voluntarily choose to participate, without "coercion or undue influence" (45 CFR 46.116, 2001). This means that subjects can be given token compensation for participating, but it cannot be inordinate. Also, and perhaps more relevant for educators, subjects must be invited to participate in such a way that they do not feel any overt or covert coercion. In a learning environment, be it college or PreK–12 school or adult learning center, the instructor is in a position of authority over the student, and whether or not students are minors, they are vulnerable to coercion by virtue of their status. The researcher should take every precaution to eliminate even the perception of coercion. At the college level, this means that the researcher cannot ask subjects directly to participate, but can advertise on campus, through oral or printed invitations disseminated by instructors.

If a researcher is also the teacher of record of the class he or she wishes to investigate, it is advisable for someone else to issue the invitation to students and collect consent forms (which should be done in such a way that no one can identify who has consented). For example, if the teacher researcher wanted to trace her graduate students' familiarity and facility with online instruction through their online journals, she could ask a colleague to come into the classroom and invite students to participate, explain the study, and collect consent forms. The colleague would keep the consent forms locked up until the term was over, so that students' choice of whether to participate would in no way affect the grades given. At that point, the colleague would give the teacher researcher the consent forms, and she could retrieve the journals of those students who had given consent, delete or disguise personal identifiers, and proceed with the analysis.

At the elementary and secondary level, parents can be given a letter (translated into the native language, if necessary) inviting them to read about the study and decide whether their child can participate. It should be made clear, of course, that the parents' permission and the students' assent are completely voluntary and will not affect the provision of services or the student's grades or status in the school.

Consent forms. Consent forms should be written in very simple language. When I did research at a community college for my dissertation, the IRB suggested that I aim at a fourth-grade reading level when choosing vocabulary, sentence length, and sentence complexity. This may sound extreme, but given the fact that most laypeople are not accustomed to the language of research, it was very good advice. Consent forms are not meant to impress the IRB; they are meant to communicate, as clearly and as simply as possible, the basic facts about the research and the participants' rights (see Appendix C [p. 79] for a sample consent form).

According to 45 CFR 42.116(a) (2001), consent forms must contain the following elements:

1. A statement that the study involves research, an explanation of the purposes of the research and the expected duration of the subject's participation, a description of the procedures to be followed, and identification of any procedures which are experimental.
2. A description of any reasonably foreseeable risks or discomforts to the subject.
3. A description of any benefits to the subject or to others which may reasonably be expected from the research.
4. A disclosure of appropriate alternative procedures or courses of treatment, if any, that might be advantageous to the subject.
5. A statement describing the extent, if any, to which confidentiality of records identifying the subject will be maintained.
6. For research involving more than minimal risk, an explanation as to whether any compensation and an explanation as to whether any medical treatments are available if injury occurs and, if so, what they consist of, or where further information may be obtained.
7. An explanation of whom to contact for answers to pertinent questions about the research and research subjects' rights, and whom to contact in the event of a research-related injury to the subject.
8. A statement that participation is voluntary, refusal to participate will involve no penalty or loss of benefits to which the subject is otherwise entitled, and the subject may discontinue participation at any time without penalty or loss of benefits to which the subject is otherwise entitled.

Additional elements may be requested by the IRB (45 CFR 46.116(b), 2001), but these are not generally applicable to educational research.

If your consent form is to be read by someone whose first language is not English, you must provide a good translation of the letter to the IRB. Subjects should be given copies of the signed consent form to keep for future reference. If your subjects are not literate, then you can read to them a short oral version of the consent form in the presence of a witness, who then signs the official consent form and the short form (45 CFR 46.117(b)(2), 2001). You can also ask the IRB to waive the consent form if subjects' signature on the form is the only record that connects them to the study and if the study presents minimal risk (45 CFR 46.117 (c)(1)(2), 2001). If the IRB waives the consent, and if subjects do not wish to sign the consent form, they can instead be given an "information form" that resembles a consent form without the signature line (Appendix D, p. 81).

As I read back over these procedures, I am reminded of the first time I wrote an IRB proposal. I must have soaked the paper with my sweat, and having submitted it, waited in dread for what I was sure would be the IRB's disapproval and their disdain of my ignorance of research! The language seemed so foreign, I was not sure what they were looking for, and reading the principal investigator's manual was like reading Greek backward. Now, having read dozens of proposals, both good and bad, I can list the most common problems that we have found with them:

1. They are poorly written, poorly edited, poorly proofread. There are discrepancies between the objectives, procedures, and supporting documentation. For example, someone may say that they will interview subjects, but no interview schedule is attached, or a survey is attached instead.
2. We cannot tell what the study's purpose is to be.
3. The research design appears to be invalid. While it is not the IRB's job to comment on a research topic, if the design is so flawed as to be useless and validity is compromised, then the IRB is within its rights to reject the study (Department of Health and Human Services, [b]).
4. We cannot tell how subjects are being selected and so cannot say whether selection is fair. If subjects are selected "by convenience," as in the case of the teacher wishing to do research with her own students, then this should be plainly stated.
5. Researchers say, "There is no risk." However, nothing is without risk. Instead, we prefer that they say, if it is true, "risk is minimal" (in other words, not greater than the risk encountered in everyday life), explain why, and say how they have minimized it.
6. We are not sure how the researcher intends to protect subjects' private information that could be used to identify them, including names, ethnicity, age, and place of residence or employment.

Special Cases

Cooperative studies. If you are working with a research partner affiliated with another institution, each institution is responsible for protecting the rights and welfare of the subjects. To save time and resources, the two cooperating institutions are allowed by the CFR to enter into a joint review agreement or rely upon the review of one or the other IRB. However, in ten years of sitting on an IRB, I have yet to see such an agreement. Most institutions simply prefer to have their own IRB review every study for which they are responsible. Our local school board not only prefers to do its own reviews but also has more stringent rules than the federal guidelines regarding research with children. Researchers need to know ahead of time what each IRB's procedures and policies are. Whatever the case, the researcher cannot recruit subjects, distribute consent forms, or collect data until all of the concerned IRBs have given approval and have one another's approval letters on file.

Doing research in another country. Collaborative international studies are flourishing now, especially in this day of virtual communication. One of my former Japanese colleagues and I were working toward a grant that would have involved a simultaneous study of Japanese learners of English in Japan and Latino learners of English in New York. Although the grant fell through, I did learn some things about how I would have proceeded. First, all federally funded research must have IRB approval both from the U.S. institution and from the foreign IRB or an equivalent board. If you are collaborating with someone whose institution does not have a sister IRB, then you can search to see whether there is an IRB in that country on register with the U.S. Office for Human Research Protections (OHRP) (http://ohrp.cit.nih.gov/search/asearch.asp#ASUR). In the case of non-funded research, you must demonstrate that the study is being conducted with sufficient knowledge of the local research context. This can be done in three ways: (1) again, have a local IRB review the protocols; (2) have a consultant from the foreign country review the protocols; or (3) have a U.S. consultant familiar with that local context do the review (OHRP, personal communication, May 3, 2004).

What if your institution does not have an IRB? If your school system or college does not have an IRB, you have several options (Department of Health and Human Services, [c]). First, you could negotiate with another institution that does have an IRB. For example, if you are doing research with another teacher or professor whose institution has an IRB, that institution might be willing to review your studies (possibly for a fee). Also, the OHRP has a list of all of its registered IRBs. You can contact one of them to see whether they would be willing to review your work (http://ohrp.cit.nih.gov/search/asearch.asp#ASUR). You can also establish your own IRB and register it with the OHRP. Finally, you can ask a commercial or an independent IRB to review your research. Any of these cases will require that you document a written "assurance" between the other IRB and your institution and that copies of this assurance be kept on file at both places (http://www.hhs.gov/ohrp/assurances/assurances_index. html#submission).

Ethical Teaching Strategies: Research in Schools

Research on children and learning is vital to the education profession; however, the regulations governing the collection of data from minors are quite complex. As an example, let's take one type of low-risk study that often causes confusion: a study that gathers data via surveys or interviews with no names or personal identifiers attached. For adults, such a study would be considered exempt. They would not need to complete a consent form, though they should receive an information form about the study (see Appendix D, p. 81). On the other hand, a study in which children (under the age of eighteen) are going to be surveyed or interviewed cannot be called exempt. It always falls in the expedited category and almost always requires parental or guardian permission, as well as child assent (see below). To make things even more complex, the IRB can waive the consent form if four conditions are met:

1. the research presents no more than minimal risk to subjects
2. waiving the consent form will not adversely affect subjects' rights and welfare
3. the research cannot be reasonably performed without the waiver
4. subjects will be provided with appropriate information afterward (45 CFR 46.116, 2001)

In one of my research projects involving the observation of classrooms designed to meet the needs of long-term ESL students, it was virtually impossible to obtain parental permission and child assent for a number of reasons (high truancy rates being one). The study was very low risk, as I did not know the students' names and only identified them as "Girl 7" or "Boy 4" in "an urban high school," so the IRB waived the consent form requirement.

However, since its passage into law in 2002, the No Child Left Behind Act has added some constraints to child research, via the Tiahrt Amendment to the Protection of Pupil Rights Amendment (PPRA; 20 USC § 1232h). The original PPRA required written parental consent before any Department of Education–related survey could be administered to students that asked for certain types of information (information that the bill's sponsors felt might invade the family's privacy). In addition, the Tiahrt Amendment to the PPRA (2002) requires that all public elementary and secondary schools develop policies regarding the rights of parents to read any surveys, instructional materials, or instruments used to collect personal information that are distributed to their children. Before you do research in schools, it is vital to find out what their current policy is. If your university IRB has deemed a survey "low risk" and "not requiring parental consent," the school IRB may now require you to obtain written consent and show the survey to each parent for approval.

Parental Permission and Child Assent

Parental or guardian permission is normally required for any research involving children and must be documented on a written consent form (45 CFR 46.117, 2001), with the exceptions mentioned above. Children who are physically and cognitively mature enough to understand the nature of the study must also give their assent to participate: either verbal assent for very young children or written assent for older children. They cannot merely "go along" and not resist the researcher's request. For younger children, the researcher should write out a simple oral explanation that will be read to the child, describing the study and asking for his or her participation. The IRB can take a judgment call about what is "too young" to assent. For older children and adolescents, it is preferable that they give written assent; for convenience's sake, they may sign the same consent form as their parents, though the explanation that they read should be written at their level. When audiotaping children (or adults, for that matter), some IRBs will ask that a separate signature line be used for the audiotaping, since it places their privacy more at risk than simply participating in the study itself. Appendix C (p. 79) shows a consent form for middle school children that also asks for permission to audiotape.

Videotaping is extremely problematic when it comes to protection of human subjects because it places their identity, privacy, and safety at greater risk than almost any other data collection instrument. This applies particularly to children. Our IRB actively discourages (though it does not ban) researchers from using videotape as a tool if other means of data collection can be found. If a researcher wishes to videotape a class, he or she will need parental or guardian permission and child assent for every child who will be videotaped. If researchers intend on showing the video at conferences, then that should be made explicit in the consent form. If some parents do not wish for their children to be videotaped or do not wish to have their child's face on a video that is shown to strangers, then their verbal interactions have to be deleted completely from the transcription, and their faces disguised. This is extremely costly and time consuming, but it can be done.

Graduate Students

Graduate student research is so important to teacher educators that we put up with a lot to see it happen. We wade through reviews of literature until our eyes are bleary, we struggle to help them understand research designs and data collection instruments, and we feel the highs and lows with them as their results begin to surface. Whatever the topic of their inquiry, it is important that graduate students understand the importance of abiding by federal regulations on the treatment of human subjects, not just as a way to avoid getting into trouble but because it is the right thing to do. While the federal government does not distinguish between professional and student researchers collecting data from human subjects (45 CFR 46.102(f), 2001), not all student research is "designed to develop or contribute to generalizable knowledge" (45 CFR 46.102(d), 2001). Your university may make a distinction, as does ours, between research practice activities and real research projects (*CUNY policy*, June 26, 2006):

(a) First, students might engage in research practica, which are really classroom exercises or student projects done in the classroom setting or in a public place to teach students how to perform certain types of data collection and analysis. They are extremely low-risk and only involve anonymous data collection. A research practicum assignment does not have to be reviewed by the IRB, but its data cannot be presented at conferences or used for publication or in a doctoral dissertation later on. If the faculty member or student anticipates using the data for one of these purposes, he or she must obtain prior IRB approval.

(b) Second, students might do research projects (directed or independent, undergraduate or honors theses, master's projects and theses, or doctoral dissertations). Student research projects, at least in our university, must be reviewed by the local IRB in the same way as faculty or administrator research.

Synthesis of Ethical Lessons Learned

Every IRB is different. Some are very strict; others are lenient. Regardless of its character, though, the fastest way to make your IRB unhappy is to lie about what you have been doing. Be honest if you have made a mistake; own up to it. It is better to throw out data that you collected without IRB approval than to jeopardize your career and your reputation. Once someone has been involved in what the federal regulations term, in their own inimitable and understated prose, "a non-compliance event," that person must submit to remediation in the form of tests, readings, and closer supervision by the IRB (such as full committee reviews) for subsequent research projects over a set probationary period. It is easier and faster to get approval to begin with.

The problem is that most of us, as teachers, are extremely busy and when ideas come to us to gather data on a particular issue, it is already halfway through the term. It can make you want to write textbooks for a living! There are two possible solutions. First, if you have in your office, as I do, reams of student course work from previous semesters, it is possible to request permission to use them as "existing data," as long as two conditions are met: (1) these documents were created by students in the normal process of teaching and not with the intention on your part of doing research, and (2) names and other personal identifiers (such as the names of schools where they work or their students) have been removed. This study would be categorized as "Exempt, 4" (Appendix A, p.76). Any IRB worth its salt will see through any attempt to "do research" by gathering data, then pretending that it was collected via normal educational practices and trying to get it treated as existing data, so do not try that. The other option for low-risk studies is to create a general proposal about a topic that you wish to investigate, and then submit changes as they come up as minor amendments.

Conclusions

To conclude, the IRB and the educational researcher should be working in tandem: the researcher to explore the fields of interest or need, the IRB to ensure that protections for human subjects are in place. The IRB should never find itself impinging on a researcher's academic freedom by rejecting a study on the basis of its topic (is it too controversial?) or because of potential misuses of the results. IRB decisions should be based only on an analysis of the research methods, the risk–benefit ratio, and the protection of human subjects (Department of Health and Human Services, [c]). Likewise, with information and preparation, the researcher can develop a good working relationship with the IRB and meet its demands in a timely fashion so as to proceed with the work at hand.

Questions for Consideration

Imagine some of your colleagues protesting that the constraints of protection for human subjects are impeding their efforts to do research and impinging on their academic freedom. After reading this chapter, how would you explain to them the rationale for complying with the federal regulations for the protection of human subjects?

With a partner, design a research project that would be conducted in your institution. Using the information in this chapter, create an IRB proposal and consent forms. What issues of protection of human subjects come up and how have you addressed them?

What are some of the privacy issues that you need to be sensitive to in your own research, be it classroom action research or research for publication?

Supplementary Resources

Reflecting on Abuses of Human Subjects in Research: Washington, H. A. (2006). *Medical apartheid: The dark history of medical experimentation on black Americans from colonial times to the present.* New York: Doubleday. At first glance, this history of medical experimentation on African Americans, at once horrific and enlightening to read, may not seem relevant to a discussion about ethics in education. However, it is a cautionary tale to anyone who would undertake research on human subjects about the tragic consequences of personal and social blind spots and about the vital need for outside, objective accountability. That alone makes this book worth reading.

Integrating Lessons on Ethics into the Classroom: Berlin, E., & Fab, J. [Directors], Fab, J. [Writer], *Paperclips.* (2004). [Documentary; DVD format]. This deeply moving, award-winning documentary begins in a rural Tennessee middle school. One of the school's social studies classes decides that to be able to visualize the enormity of the Holocaust, they will collect a paperclip for every person murdered under the Nazi regime. What ensues will change their lives and that of their town forever. This documentary is a powerful reminder of what happens when we treat others as objects rather than as subjects. It is appropriate for middle school and up.

References

Anderson, G., with Arsenaut, N. (1998). *Fundamentals of educational research.* Philadelphia: Routledge.

Application for approval to use human subjects in research. (n.d.). Bronx, NY: Lehman College, the City University of New York. Retrieved February 6, 2007, from http://www.lehman.edu/provost/irb.

Belmont Report: *Ethical principles and guidelines for the protection of human subjects of research.* (1979). Bethesda, MD: The National Institutes of Health, the National Commission for the Protection of Human Subjects of Biomedical and Behavioral Research.

Code of Federal Regulations. 45 CFR § 46.102, 116, 117 (2001).

CUNY policy for student research with human subjects. (June 26, 2006). New York: The City University of New York. Retrieved February 1, 2006, from www.rfcuny.org/ResCompliance/Student_Research.html.

Department of Health and Human Services. (a). *Human research questions and answers: What if my institution does not have an internal institutional review board*

(IRB) or independent ethics committee (IEC)? Retrieved February 7, 2007, from http://answers.ohrp.hhs.gov/cgi-bin/answers_ohrp.cfg/php/enduser.

———. (b). *Institutional review board guidebook*, chapter III, "Risk and Benefit Analysis," "Informed Consent." Retrieved January 30, 2007, from www.hhs.gov/ohrp.irb.

———. (c). *Institutional review board guidebook*, chapter V, "Behavioral Research." Retrieved January 30, 2007, from www.hhs.gov/ohrp.irb.

Gordon, E. J. (2003). Trials and tribulations of navigating IRBs: Anthropological and biomedical perspectives of "risk" in conducting human subjects research. *Anthropological Quarterly, 76*(2), 299–320.

Jones, J. H. (1993). *Bad blood: The Tuskegee syphilis experiment.* Northampton, MA: Free Press.

Lathrop, V. G. (1983). Careful review, not bureaucratic delay. *IRB: Ethics and Human Research, 5*(4), 9–10.

Levine, M. (1983). IRB review as a "cooling out" device. *IRB: Ethics and Human Research, 5*(4), 8–9.

Nuremberg Code. (1949). Reprinted from *Trials of war criminals before the Nuremberg Military Tribunals under control Council law No. 10*, vol. 2 (pp. 181–182). Washington, DC: U.S. Government Printing Office. Retrieved January 28, 2007, from http://ohsr.od.nih.gov.guidelines.nuremberg.html.

Pritchard, I. A. (2002). Travelers and trolls: Practitioner research and institutional review boards. *Educational Researcher, 31*(3), 3–13.

Tiahrt Amendment to the Protection of Pupil Rights Amendment. 20 U.S.C. § 1232h (2002).

Tsai, D. F. (1999). Ancient Chinese medical ethics and the four principles of biomedical ethics. *Journal of Medical Ethics, 25*(4), 315–321.

Veatch, R. M., & Mason, C. G. (1987). Hippocratic vs. Judeo-Christian medical ethics: Principles in conflict. *Journal of Religious Ethics, 15*(1), 86–105.

Washington, H. A. (2006). *Medical apartheid: The dark history of medical experimentation on black Americans from colonial times to the present.* New York: Doubleday.

Appendix A

Exemption Categories
(45 CFR 46, Subpart A, 46.101)
(http://www.hhs.gov/ohrp/humansubjects/guidance/45cfr46.htm)

1. Research conducted in established or commonly accepted educational settings, involving normal educational practices, such as (i) research on regular and special education instructional strategies, or (ii) research on the effectiveness of or the comparison among instructional techniques, curricula, or classroom management methods.
2. Research involving the use of educational tests (cognitive, diagnostic, aptitude, achievement), survey procedures, interview procedures, or observation of public behavior, unless (i) information obtained is recorded in such a manner that human subjects can be identified, directly or through identifiers linked to the subjects; and (ii) any disclosure of the human subjects' responses outside the research could reasonably place the subjects at risk of criminal or civil liability or be damaging to the subjects' financial standing, employability, or reputation.
3. Research involving the use of educational tests (cognitive, diagnostic, aptitude, achievement), survey procedures, interview procedures, or observation of public behavior that is not exempt under paragraph (b)(2) of this section, if: (i) the human subjects are elected or appointed public officials or candidates for public office; or (ii) federal statute(s) require(s) without exception that the confidentiality of the personally identifiable information will be maintained throughout the research and thereafter.
4. Research involving the collection or study of existing data, documents, records, pathological specimens, or diagnostic specimens, if these sources are publicly available or if the information is recorded by the investigator in such a manner that subjects cannot be identified, directly or through identifiers linked to the subjects.
5. Research and demonstration projects which are conducted by or subject to the approval of department or agency heads, and which are designed to study, evaluate, or otherwise examine: (i) Public benefit or service programs; (ii) procedures for obtaining benefits or services under those programs; (iii) possible changes in or alternatives to those programs or procedures; or (iv) possible changes in methods or levels of payment for benefits or services under those programs.
6. Taste and food quality evaluation and consumer acceptance studies, (i) if wholesome foods without additives are consumed or (ii) if a food is consumed that contains a food ingredient at or below the level and for a use

found to be safe, or agricultural chemical or environmental contaminant at or below the level found to be safe, by the Food and Drug Administration or approved by the Environmental Protection Agency or the Food Safety and Inspection Service of the U.S. Department of Agriculture.

Appendix B

Expedited Categories
(45 CFR 46, Subpart A, 46.110)
(http://www.hhs.gov/ohrp/humansubjects/guidance/expedited98.htm)

1. Clinical studies of drugs and medical devices only when condition (a) or (b) is met.
   (a) Research on drugs for which an investigational new drug application (21 CFR Part 312) is not required. (Note: Research on marketed drugs that significantly increases the risks or decreases the acceptability of the risks associated with the use of the product is not eligible for expedited review.)
   (b) Research on medical devices for which (i) an investigational device exemption application (21 CFR Part 812) is not required; or (ii) the medical device is cleared/approved for marketing and the medical device is being used in accordance with its cleared/approved labeling.
2. Collection of blood samples by finger stick, heel stick, ear stick, or venipuncture as follows:
   (a) from healthy, nonpregnant adults who weigh at least 110 pounds. For these subjects, the amounts drawn may not exceed 550 ml in an 8 week period and collection may not occur more frequently than 2 times per week; or
   (b) from other adults and children, considering the age, weight, and health of the subjects, the collection procedure, the amount of blood to be collected, and the frequency with which it will be collected. For these subjects, the amount drawn may not exceed the lesser of 50 ml or 3 ml per kg in an 8 week period and collection may not occur more frequently than 2 times per week.
3. Prospective collection of biological specimens for research purposes by noninvasive means.
   Examples: (a) hair and nail clippings in a nondisfiguring manner; (b) deciduous teeth at time of exfoliation or if routine patient care indicates a need for extraction; (c) permanent teeth if routine patient care indicates a need for extraction; (d) excreta and external

secretions (including sweat); (e) uncannulated saliva collected either in an unstimulated fashion or stimulated by chewing gumbase or wax or by applying a dilute citric solution to the tongue; (f) placenta removed at delivery; (g) amniotic fluid obtained at the time of rupture of the membrane prior to or during labor; (h) supra- and subgingival dental plaque and calculus, provided the collection procedure is not more invasive than routine prophylactic scaling of the teeth and the process is accomplished in accordance with accepted prophylactic techniques; (i) mucosal and skin cells collected by buccal scraping or swab, skin swab, or mouth washings; (j) sputum collected after saline mist nebulization.

4. Collection of data through noninvasive procedures (not involving general anesthesia or sedation) routinely employed in clinical practice, excluding procedures involving x-rays or microwaves. Where medical devices are employed, they must be cleared/approved for marketing. (Studies intended to evaluate the safety and effectiveness of the medical device are not generally eligible for expedited review, including studies of cleared medical devices for new indications.)

Examples: (a) physical sensors that are applied either to the surface of the body or at a distance and do not involve input of significant amounts of energy into the subject or an invasion of the subject's privacy; (b) weighing or testing sensory acuity; (c) magnetic resonance imaging; (d) electrocardiography, electroencephalography, thermography, detection of naturally occurring radioactivity, electroretinography, ultrasound, diagnostic infrared imaging, doppler blood flow, and echocardiography; (e) moderate exercise, muscular strength testing, body composition assessment, and flexibility testing where appropriate given the age, weight, and health of the individual.

5. Research involving materials (data, documents, records, or specimens) that have been collected, or will be collected solely for nonresearch purposes (such as medical treatment or diagnosis). (NOTE: Some research in this category may be exempt from the HHS regulations for the protection of human subjects. 45 CFR 46.101(b)(4). This listing refers only to research that is not exempt.)

6. Collection of data from voice, video, digital, or image recordings made for research purposes.

7. Research on individual or group characteristics or behavior (including, but not limited to, research on perception, cognition, motivation, identity, language, communication, cultural beliefs or practices, and social behavior) or research employing survey, interview, oral history, focus

group, program evaluation, human factors evaluation, or quality assurance methodologies. (NOTE: Some research in this category may be exempt from the HHS regulations for the protection of human subjects. 45 CFR 46.101(b)(2) and (b)(3). This listing refers only to research that is not exempt.)

8. Continuing review of research previously approved by the convened IRB as follows:
   (a) where (i) the research is permanently closed to the enrollment of new subjects; (ii) all subjects have completed all research-related interventions; and (iii) the research remains active only for long-term follow-up of subjects; or
   (b) where no subjects have been enrolled and no additional risks have been identified; or
   (c) where the remaining research activities are limited to data analysis.

9. Continuing review of research, not conducted under an investigational new drug application or investigational device exemption where categories two (2) through eight (8) do not apply but the IRB has determined and documented at a convened meeting that the research involves no greater than minimal risk and no additional risks have been identified.

Appendix C

Sample Consent Form for Working with Minors and Audiotaping

Consent Form

Investigator:	**Institutional Contact:**
Name (Ms. X)	Name, IRB Coordinator (Ms. Y)
Dept./College or School	Hall, Room
Mailing Address	College
City, State, Zip	City, State, Zip
Your phone and email address	Phone and email address

Dear Parent or Guardian:

Ms. X is a teacher at _____ Middle School. She is inviting your child to be a part of a study on things that affect how well children do on math tests. The study is described below. If you and your child agree to participate, please sign the next page and return the form to Ms. X.

Study Description:

Ms. X is interested in finding out whether worry, lack of sleep, and nutrition affect how well students do on the City middle school math test. Your child was selected because he/she is taking the City math test this year. If you give your child permission to participate and if your child agrees to participate, then he or she will be given a survey after completing the City math test. This survey will take about 20 minutes to complete. Your child may also be selected to do a 10-minute interview with the researcher about his or her feelings about the mathematics test. The interview will be audiotaped so that the researcher can play it back and write down what your child says accurately.

Your Rights, Privacy, and Welfare:

1. In order to ensure that your child's answers remain confidential, the survey will be numbered and all personal information removed. No one will know which students completed the survey except for the researcher.
2. The audiotaped interviews will also be coded so that no one will know who your child is. The researcher is the only one who will listen to the tapes, and she will not identify your child in the transcriptions or in her study. She will destroy the tapes when she is finished.
3. You are free to withdraw your consent and your child is free to discontinue participation in any part of this study at any time. He or she does not have to answer any questions that he or she prefers not to answer. This will not affect his or her grade in any way.
4. If you or your child has questions about the study, please contact Ms. X. If you or your child has questions about his or her rights as a participant, please contact Ms. Y.

Parent/Guardian:

I have read this consent form and I understand the procedures to be used in this study. I freely and voluntarily allow my child to participate. I understand that he/she may discontinue his/her participation at any time without penalty.

Parent/Guardian's Name (please print):_____

Signature:_____

Date:_____

I understand that my child may be selected for an interview with the researcher and that this interview will be audiotaped. I freely and voluntarily agree to allow my child to be audiotaped. I understand that my child may discontinue his or her participation at any time without penalty.

Parent/Guardian's Name (please print):_____
Signature:_____
Date:_____

Student:

I have read this consent form, and I know what I am going to do for this study. I want to participate. I understand that I may drop out of the study at any time.

Student's Name (please print):_____
Signature:_____
Date:_____

I know that I may be selected for an interview with the researcher. I agree to let her tape the interview. I understand that I may stop the interview at any time.

Student's Name (please print):_____
Signature:_____
Date:_____

Appendix D

Sample Information Form for Exempt Studies (No Signature)

Information Form

Investigator:	**Institutional Contact:**
Name (Ms. X)	Name, IRB Coordinator (Ms. Y)
Dept./College or School	Hall, Room
Mailing Address	College
City, State, Zip	City, State, Zip
Your phone and email address	Phone and email address

Dear Teacher,

Ms. X, a graduate student at _____ College, would like to invite you to participate in a study about the connection between teacher expectations and student academic achievement.

Study Description:

If you agree to participate, please complete the attached anonymous questionnaire and return it to the investigator in the attached envelope. The questionnaire should take about 5-10 minutes to complete. Please do not write your name or any other identifying information on the questionnaire or the envelope.

Your Rights, Privacy, and Welfare:

1. In order to ensure that your answers remain confidential, please do not write your name or any other identifying information on the questionnaire. In any case, the researcher will not use your name or the school's name in the report. In addition, only the researcher and her advisor will review the data, and the questionnaires will be kept in a secure cabinet after the study is completed.

2. Participation is completely voluntary. You are free to withdraw your consent and to discontinue participating in this study at any time. You do not have to answer any questions that you prefer not to answer. Your choice to participate will have no effect on your employment or status at your school. If you have any questions about the study, you can contact Ms. X at the number given above. If you have questions about your rights as a participant, you may contact Ms. Y at the number given above.

Part II

Ethical Commitment to Teacher Research

The Classroom,
the University,
the Dilemma

CR 8

RESEARCHING IN A SMALL-TOWN SCHOOL
Getting to Know Each Other

Cynthia A. Lassonde

anyone lived in a pretty how town
(with up so floating many bells down)
spring summer autumn winter
he sang his did not he danced his did.

—e. e. cummings, 1994, p. 73

Chapter Overview

- Recognizing that knowing the students we teach involves not only knowing their academic strengths and needs but understanding the personal aspects that foster and hinder learning.
- Applying research findings to life and life findings to research.
- Pros and cons of teaching in the school of a small town where you live and strategies for capitalizing on the pros and overcoming or avoiding the cons.

Inspirational Reflection

For many years, before moving to teach at the college level, I taught in a small, rural elementary school in upstate New York. It was my family's neighborhood school, the school my daughters attended. The community was a "pretty how town" much like the one I imagine e. e. cummings used for the setting of the first stanza of "Anyone Lived in a Pretty How Town," which appears as the epigraph to this chapter. In our how town, my family sang and danced our "did nots" and "dids" through the years as we moved through life together as part of a small community.

As a result of living in this small town where I taught, my family and I had close ties with many of my students' families, and I had personal and academic relationships with my colleagues. I attended events outside of school alongside the same families who frequented my classroom for conferences and holiday celebrations. In short, because I was an educator who taught and lived in a small town, my life was an open book and the lives of my students were open books to me. I felt much as I imagined the school marm in "Little House on the Prairie" must have felt. That is, I strongly felt that my home and professional lives were reflective of each other. My students were not only my charges; they were my neighbors.

You are probably wondering how research fitted into this setting. One year, while teaching fifth grade, I implemented a year-long study of how my students' social identities fostered or hindered their academic identities. This study was largely influenced by the fact that I did know my students well, and this affected how I taught and how students responded to me and to the whole learning environment.

After reading much literature to prepare for my teacher research project, I came upon a theory called positioning. Positioning theory as described by Harre and van Langenhove (1999) looks at "the necessity of paying close attention to the local moral order, the local system of rights, duties, and obligations, within which both public and private intentional acts are done" (p. 1). In a classroom setting, positioning theory is like taking on a role, but these roles are ever-changing according to whom we are with, what the situation is, what the assignment or expectations are, and who the teacher is.

I interpreted this theory to apply to my classroom through the academic and social identities my students took on in relation to how they positioned themselves among their classmates. By collecting evidence through the systematic methods of teacher research, I found that the social and academic positions (or roles) my students hoped to convey to each other and to me in certain environments did foster and/or hinder their motivation, effort, and ability to learn and to express themselves. In short, the social affected the academic and vice versa in very specific and measurable ways.

Through my teacher research study, I realized that ethical considerations become a daily way of life for the teacher both inside and outside of the classroom if the teacher hopes to ensure the "protection of freedom to learn and to teach and the guarantee of equal educational opportunity for all" (National Education Association, 1975, p. 1). To apply what is in this chapter, the reader does not have to be in the same situation in which I found myself. The context just highlighted and exacerbated the ethical issues that arose. But I propose that my research helped me to gain insight into just how important it is to be aware of the community and family lives of our students and to share part of ourselves as just plain people with our students as well. How better to create a classroom in which communication is encouraged, opinions and thoughts are respected, and mistakes are valued, forgiven, and seen as a means for learning to take place? My research provides evidence of the following challenges relating to providing equal educational opportunities through ethical decision making.

Challenges Related to Ethical Decision Making

For me as a teacher and a parent, my situation was challenging in several ways. First, my credibility as a professional was always under scrutiny. Not only did I have to uphold my professionalism within the classroom, but I wanted to maintain a high moral standard for my family and students within the community. This meant big things, such as not having a beer in my hand at a picnic that included anyone from the neighborhood, as well as little things, such as making sure my dog did not tear the neighbor's garbage apart. You may think these are exaggerated or humorous examples, but I can assure you that they are real examples of things I thought about from day to day. I saw myself as a model and mentor for not only my own children but for my students. How could I teach them not to drink and how could I invite the local sheriff into my classroom to talk about the dangers of drugs and alcohol if I had been seen drinking even one beer myself? Fortunately, if you know me, you will know this issue was not a great sacrifice for me. But this vein of thought follows through with being concerned about supporting a particular political candidate publicly, voicing my opinion about school district issues, and even the clothes my daughters wore to school.

The second challenge I would like to share concerns the equality of the relationships I had with my students. Obviously, as a community member, I knew some families better than others. I had three daughters in the same school, so I knew their friends better than others just by virtue of the sheer amount of time they spent with my daughters. So I had to be very careful not to have "favorites" or even to spend more time with some students than others. I certainly did not want my students to feel less important or less liked by me than my daughters' friends were.

The final challenge I would like to share relates to advocating for my students, which, at times, meant disagreeing with colleagues who did not know my students as well as I did. Or, in some cases, they knew them or their families' reputations as community members, but they did not know the children as students. There were instances over the years when fellow teachers or teaching aides misinterpreted students' intentions or actions. Students came to me to share their point of view, and there were times when I brought these students to the other adult and helped the student explain his or her side or motivation. I remember one colleague credited me with always standing up for the students. I usually took the students' word as truth until it was proven untrue. And I always took the time to listen to students' perspectives because sometimes, I found, they had misinterpreted or misunderstood events or comments. I felt students should be heard. Many, in their minds, were right and did not understand why they were being accused of wrongdoing. By advocating for them, I tried to show them they were respected as people, and I tried to make the situation a learning experience rather than a the-adult-is-always-right mandate. However, I am sure there were colleagues who felt I was questioning their authority in these instances.

There were other challenges. For example, my daughters sometimes were scrutinized by adults, teachers, and their peers more closely than others just because they were daughters of a teacher in the school. Also, it was difficult to share the "bad news" with some families because I felt I had failed them and their children not only as a teacher but as a friend. Yet, keep in mind that this section is meant to share the challenges, not to complain about the disadvantages. I see challenges in a positive light. Challenges make us who we are. It's how we face the challenges in our lives that turns them into positive learning experiences.

Ethical Teaching Strategies

My research helped me to become a more effective teacher. It not only allowed me to take a close look at the teaching and learning environment but also highlighted the interactions among my students and myself and how the positions students took influenced their learning. Therefore, the first action that helped me face the challenges that surrounded me was to plan and execute the teacher research project previously described. My research encouraged me to talk with my students, colleagues, and students' families to expand on their thoughts and perspectives. When something emerged from my qualitative data that did not make sense to me, I would follow it through and ask clarifying questions. After reflecting on data, such as my teacher journal and family interviews, as I collected it, I would sometimes note something I had missed in real time. And, finally, there were times when writing about my observations that the writing act would reveal something to me I did not realize was happening. I relate this to the idea that writing can act to "hold thinking still" (Haneda & Wells, 2000, p. 431), to encourage analytic reflection.

Next, I would like to suggest strategies for facing the challenges I described in the previous section. The first was upholding my credibility as a professional.

How responsible is a teacher for being a model of moral ethics for her students outside of the classroom? I think this is very important. When we become teachers, we do so in all walks of life. If we don't want to take that on, we should not become teachers. Students should look up to a teacher as someone of whom they are proud to say, "She's my teacher." Much like a clergyman or a politician, I think our profession comes with responsibilities to be accountable for our actions wherever we are. However, there is a line we can draw in the sand to separate home from school. That line, I have found, comes after having gained our students' respect. The line, I maintain, should remain moral. For example, there are times when I say to my students, "I have my opinions just like you do. But I wouldn't expect you to change your opinion just because it's different from mine. However, I would want you to respect it and listen to it just as I would want to listen to yours. I may not agree with you, and you may not agree with me. But we can learn from each other's opinions." This line of professional morality should reflect respect and open communication.

The second challenge mentioned previously was about the equality of my relationships with my students. I have kept a checklist of students' names on my desk just to make sure I spent ten minutes per week just chatting with each student about events outside of the classroom. I would start the conversation with, "So, what's up with you lately?" Or, if I had seen them at the local store or in town, I would ask, "What were you up to yesterday?" I took time during lunch to sit with groups of students on a regular basis just for a couple of minutes (because I felt lunch time should be a chance for them to relax and talk with their peers, and, to tell the truth, I usually could not stand the cafeteria noise longer than that). Or I would have groups of students up to my classroom to have lunch with me. We also would plan together days when we would come to lunch in the classroom and have "lunch and a movie." In short, there were planned times when I made an effort to just relate to each student in a personal way so each felt he or she was my "favorite." To avoid any problems, I would recommend that a teacher never meet with a student in the classroom alone, however. I always make sure I have at least two students in the room if I am helping them with work or just chatting. If no one else is around when a student stops by, just ask the student to step out into the hall. In cases when the student wants to confide something in private, always keep the door open. This is something that was recommended to me by my first principal, and I think it is wise advice.

Finally, the third challenge relates to advocating for students in situations that sometimes involve confronting colleagues. This can be tricky. My strategy is first to talk with the student, and then to talk with the adult involved, to get both sides of the story. If possible, I would also talk with witnesses. When talking with the adult, I would relate the student's side of the situation to the adult and then request a time when the three of us could get together if needed. If the student did not feel comfortable facing the adult, I would sometimes allow him or her to write a letter to the adult explaining what happened. You have to be careful when you take this position as student advocate to ensure that the students do not start to see you as a way to get out of trouble. There have been cases in which students have told me stories that were unsupported by others. Try to maintain a neutral position between the adult and student so neither thinks you are taking sides. I saw my role as someone who allowed the student to voice his or her point of view in an effort to clarify misunderstandings. I did not judge.

Synthesis of Ethical Lessons Learned

Being an integral part of my students' lives outside of school allowed me to gain their trust as well as their families' trust, helped me relate to their interests and prior understandings with deep insight, and opened doors of communication that fostered advanced progress.

My teacher research project helped me bridge the gap between my ethical decision making and my philosophical approach in that the results helped me reflect on the importance of listening to students' and families' voices. I realized how advantageous it is for a teacher to hear the personal voices to advocate for the academic progress of his or her students. The challenges of completing this project in my classroom involved taking a critical look at how my colleagues' responses to my students influenced their learning, how family perspectives affected students' ability and motivation to participate, and how my perceived relationship with my students and their families helped to determine students' academic identities.

Although not all readers will be in the same small-town situation that I describe in this chapter, I believe the implications and strategies are on target for all teachers. The chapter synthesizes the ethical lessons I learned in dealing with students, families, and colleagues in ways that protected and enhanced my own sought-after identities as an upstanding educator and citizen.

Questions for Consideration

As a student: Have you ever been a student in a classroom where you felt the teacher either "really got you" or did not know you or care to know you at all? What were these learning experiences like?

As a teacher or future teacher: In what ways would you try or have you tried to incorporate what you know about your students into their learning experience?

If you were a teacher in a small town, what parts of your life or activities would you like to keep private and what would you share with your community (potential students and families of students)? Where would you draw your "line in the sand" between these worlds?

Supplementary Resources

Cuilla, J. B., & Burns, J. M. (2004). *Ethics, the heart of leadership.* Westport, CT: Greenwood Publishing Group. Although this book focuses on ethics in business, it offers chapters on being an ethical leader. Topics such as trust and empowerment are presented in a way that can easily be applied to education settings.

Goldstein, L. S. (2002). *Reclaiming caring in teaching and teacher education.* New York: Peter Lang. What does it mean to be a caring teacher? This resource discusses the challenges caring teachers might face and how to overcome these challenges.

Sparks, D. (2004). *Leading for results: Transforming teaching, learning, and relationships in schools.* Thousand Oaks, CA: Sage. Before teaching ethics in the classroom, teachers should first clarify their values and positions on critical issues. This book guides teachers in how to do just that and then presents strategies to help students find their truths, make and keep promises, and stand up for their points of view in productive ways.

References

cummings, e. e. (1994). Anyone lived in a pretty how town. In *One hundred selected poems* (p. 73). Berkley, CA: Grove/Atlantic (original poem written in 1940).

Haneda, M., & Wells, G. (2000). Writing in knowledge-building communities. *Research in the Teaching of English, 34,* 430–457.

Harre, R., & van Langenhove, L. (Eds.). (1999). *Positioning theory: Moral contexts of intentional action.* Malden, MA: Blackwell.

National Education Association. (1975). *Code of ethics of the education profession.* Retrieved July 6, 2006, from http://www.nea.org/aboutnea/code.htm.

CR 9

REFLECTIONS ON A DILEMMA IN SPECIAL EDUCATION COURSES

Nithya Narayanaswamy Iyer and Daqi Li

> We cannot make it rain, but we can see to it that it falls on prepared soil.
> —*Henri J. M. Nouwen (1932–1996), 1980*

Chapter Overview

- What are the effects of the ethical issues in special education on pre-service teacher training?
- How can teacher educators provide a rich learning experience for pre-service teachers without infringing upon the rights of children with disabilities?
- How do ethical standards in special education influence teacher research designs?

Inspirational Reflection

As teacher educators, we are continuously seeking ways to help teachers reach all members of their classes. We believe that people learn in different ways and that no one approach to teaching works for all students. Understanding the social and cultural background, interests, experiences, strengths, and goals that may influence a student's learning style helps us design effective curricula, pedagogy, and assessment. Valuing individual differences in student learning traits is at the core of our teaching philosophy, and we adjust our teaching to the strengths of the individual students in the classroom.

We believe teachers have a tremendous impact on their students and, ultimately, on the larger society. To be an effective teacher, it is important to prepare students to take responsibility for becoming lifelong learners. This requires students to reflect on their own learning and share their learning with others. As teacher educators, it is also important that we teach preservice teachers about diversity and difference among learners.

Our philosophy of teaching is aligned with the principles of the National Council for Accreditation of Teacher Education (NCATE). NCATE has adopted a set of standards, one of which requires that "pre-service teachers learn to develop and teach lessons that incorporate diversity and develop a classroom and school climate that values diversity" (2006, Diversity, para. 1). Furthermore, preservice teachers should be "aware of different teaching and learning styles shaped by cultural influences and be able to adapt instruction and services appropriately for all students, including students with exceptionalities" (Diversity, para. 1).

Since NCATE standards are research-based national standards for good practice in teacher education, many teacher preparation programs encourage the completion of field experience in a variety of settings, including an inclusive classroom that contains students with and without disabilities. Owing to the unique privacy issues regarding students with special needs, however, preservice teachers may encounter difficulties surrounding the challenge of identifying these children in an inclusive classroom. These difficulties may negatively affect the outcomes of preservice teachers' field experiences.

Challenges Relating to Privacy Issues

Of greatest importance when dealing with children with special needs is the ethical issue of confidentiality and privacy of information: "The fundamental intent is to protect a client's right to privacy by ensuring that matters disclosed to a professional not be relayed to others without the informed consent of the client" (Center for Mental Health in Schools, 1998). Children with special needs remain particularly vulnerable to becoming targets of humiliation, discrimination, and abuse. Educators are therefore obligated to protect the identity of children with disabilities by following guidelines and laws aimed at keeping information about these students confidential. These regulations are as follows: (1) written or oral information about these students and their families may be shared only with personnel who can benefit the student and his or her family by having this knowledge; (2) recipients should protect the information from disclosure; (3) information concerning a particular student may not be shared with other students or parents under any circumstances; and (4) discussions concerning confidential information are to take place in secured locations (Mountain Plains Regional Resource Center, 1998). When personnel such as substitutes and para-educators are in the class, the classroom teacher must inform them about the need for confidentiality. They should discuss the guidelines of confidentiality for their class and how to proceed if the classroom teacher is absent. Para-educators need to be aware that students' files should be locked up at all times and that what they observe, hear, or learn in the class should stay in the class to protect the rights of these children (Fleury, 2000).

In accordance with the mandates specified in the Individuals with Disabilities Education Improvement Act (IDEA; 20 U.S.C. 1412 (a)), all children with disabilities must be educated in the least restrictive environment. IDEA has made it possible for many children with disabilities to attend school alongside their peers without disabilities in regular education classrooms. As a result, all teachers must receive training in teaching classes that include children with disabilities. To prepare teachers to meet this challenge better, this training should begin in preservice education programs.

Preservice teachers take courses in special education that cover the cognitive, emotional, social, physical, and motivational characteristics, as well as educational requirements, of exceptional children. The course requirement to complete a field assignment that involves hands-on experience observing and interacting in an inclusive classroom setting to learn about the needs and the challenges of educating children with special needs helps to create an environment of shared responsibility where all concerned are committed to ensuring that every child learns and approaches her or his potential. During the field experience, preservice teachers participate in academic activities and observe how classroom teachers help children who exhibit possible learning or behavior problems. However, in these inclusive classrooms, preservice teachers are considered visitors in the school building, and therefore do not have the privilege of receiving confidential information such as the identity of children with disabilities.

This need for confidentiality presents a dilemma: on the one hand, we expect our preservice teachers to learn about and better understand the challenges of teaching classes with exceptional children; on the other, since the identity of these children cannot be revealed, preservice teachers are left to attempt to figure out the information themselves.

We want preservice teachers to learn about children with special needs in authentic classroom settings, but schools and teachers are bound by powerful laws and regulations: IDEA requires that appropriate action be taken to "ensure the protection of the confidentiality of any personally identifiable data, information, and records" (20 U.S.C. 1417(c)). New York State has a similar requirement. Under the Regulations of the Commissioner of Education Part 200—Students with Disabilities, each board of education or board of trustees must adopt written policy that

> establishes administrative practices and procedures for the purpose of ensuring the confidentiality of personally identifiable data, information or records pertaining to a student with a disability. Such personally identifiable information shall not be disclosed by any officer or employee of the State Education Department or any school district, or member of a committee on special education or committee on preschool special education to any person other than the parent of such student, except in accordance with section 300.500 and sections 300.560 through 300.577 and Part 99 of title 34 of the Code of Federal Regulations. (Office of Vocational and Educational Services for Individuals with Disabilities, 2005)

This dilemma affects both preservice teachers and teacher educators. It hinders preservice teachers' understanding of the characteristics of disabilities, limiting their understanding of the special needs of children, and forces teacher educators to make compromises in the assessment of preservice teachers and to seek other venues to bridge the gap. As a result of lack of access to the identity of children with special needs, preservice teachers' reflections tend to focus on the obvious academic or behavioral problems while neglecting some of the less noticeable characteristics. Descriptions of children who are "suspected" to have a disability often appear shallow and too general, demonstrating a lack of depth of understanding. For example, preservice teachers may misinterpret typical rambunctious behaviors as ADHD or may assume that a student who appears sad or belligerent has an emotional behavioral disorder, failing to correctly identify high functional autism or a hearing impairment.

Ethical Alternatives for Preservice Teacher Training

We want our preservice teachers to have a variety of experiences so that they are prepared to be the best possible teachers they can be. Several approaches can be utilized to provide a rich learning experience for preservice teachers, including classroom observations, video cases, simulations, interviews, and reflections. During classroom observations, preservice teachers observe teachers and students in an inclusive classroom, resource room, or special education classroom, interacting with students during classroom activities, and observe how classroom teachers help those children who appear to have learning or behavior problems. Observing students with disabilities in the resource room or special education room presents an excellent opportunity for preservice teachers to learn about various disabilities and strategies employed by resource room teachers but requires close monitoring to make sure all legal issues are addressed. Gaining access to the classroom can be difficult, as it requires permission from the parents of all children in the special education environment to protect privacy. Some states may also require institutional review board approval, thus challenging colleges and universities to develop a system and protocol to ensure that applications are handled smoothly, legally, and in a timely fashion and that placement sites are cooperative and parents are willing. Also, issues such as one parent being unwilling to give consent must be addressed.

Another way preservice teachers can learn about individual education plans and various disabilities is through video cases, which help preservice teachers explore and discuss individual cases of various disabilities and possible instructional strategies that may be appropriate for the situation. In addition, simulations are an excellent way for preservice teachers to explore what it feels like to live with a disability; they have been found to shape attitudes effectively (Behler, 1993). They also lead to a better understanding of disabilities and a decrease in stereotyping of children with disabilities (Pearl, 2004). It should be cautioned that while simulations are a meaningful activity for preservice teachers to explore experiences of children with disabilities, simulation assignments carried out outside of the classroom can be difficult for instructors to assess.

Preservice teachers can also interview individuals with disabilities, helping them to examine their attitude and reflect on their reactions and responses to situations in which individuals with disabilities are involved. Another way for students to interact with individuals with disabilities and explore what it is like to live with a disability is through scenarios, requiring preservice teachers to discuss real-life situations with an individual with a disability and to describe his or her reactions and responses. This reflective activity helps preservice teachers to explore their preconceptions and to understand that certain everyday activities typically taken for granted can be quite challenging for students with disabilities. Yet, it is again challenging to assume that these interviews were real. Possibly teacher educators need to provide a pool of volunteers, including children and adults with disabilities who have been screened and are willing to be interviewed. Perhaps this process could be facilitated by a college or university student learning center.

Synthesis of Ethical Lessons Learned

Most teacher preparation programs require preservice teachers to complete field experiences in a variety of settings, including an inclusive classroom. However, schools are legally obligated to protect all children's rights in special education. Since schools and teachers are bound by confidentiality, they cannot reveal the identities of children with disabilities, and obtaining parental permission might present a challenge. A variety of field experiences, such as

general and inclusive classroom interaction and observation, video case studies, interviews, and scenarios, remain excellent ways for preservice teachers
to learn about various disabilities and strategies employed by resource room
teachers. As teacher educators, we want to provide meaningful learning experiences for our preservice teachers in hopes of providing all schools with quality
teachers.

Questions for Consideration

When you place preservice teachers in an inclusive classroom with children
with disabilities, how would you deal with the dilemma that on the one hand
you want them to learn as much as possible about the special needs of children
with disabilities but on the other you are legally and ethically obligated to with-
hold some information from them?

What alternative approaches may help resolve this problem and enhance preservice teachers' classroom observation experience?

Assessing preservice teachers' field experience fairly can be a challenge when
they are not provided with some important information about the children
they observe. As a teacher educator, what criteria would you use when assessing preservice teachers' observation of an inclusive class that has children with
disabilities?

Supplementary Resources

Goor, M. B., & Santos, K. E. (2002). *To think like a teacher: Cases for special education
interns and novice teachers.* Boston, MA: Allyn and Bacon. This text is primarily for
preservice and novice educators working with children with disabilities. Cases
are used to help readers to examine and reflect on genuine issues in special
education. Chapter 6 deals with special education procedures and legal issues.
One of the issues is confidentiality, and the illustrative case shows confidentiality is crucial in special education.

Yell, M. (2006). *The law and special education* (2nd ed.). Upper Saddle River, NJ:
Pearson Merrill Prentice Hall. This book is aimed at educators rather than individuals who practice the law. The text provides a wealth of information about
the legal development of special education and the current legal requirements
in providing education to students with disabilities. Various special education
issues are addressed, including confidentiality of student records (chapter 15).

Teaching Exceptional Children Plus. This journal publishes materials for individuals who work with children with special needs. It features articles on instruction and services for exceptional children, case studies and case theories, and book reviews. Readers can find articles in this journal that deal with legal issues in special education.

References

20 U.S.C. Individuals with Disabilities Education Improvement Act of 2004. Retrieved February 8, 2007, from http://thomas.loc.gov/cgi-bin/query/z?c108:h.r.1350.enr:.

Behler, G. T. (1993). Disability simulations as a teaching tool: Some ethical issues and implications. *Journal of Postsecondary Education and Disability, 10*(2), 3–8.

Center for Mental Health in Schools, Californian University, Los Angeles. (1998). Confidentiality and informed consent. An introductory packet. (ERIC Document ED 427 125).

Fleury, M. (2000). Confidentiality issues with substitutes and para-educators. *Teaching Exceptional Children, 33*(1), 44–45.

Mountain Plains Regional Resource Center, Utah State University, Logan. (1998). Special education issues in confidentiality. (ERIC Document ED 444 325).

NCATE. (2006). *NCATE unit standards.* Retrieved January 31, 2007, from http://www.ncate.org/public/unitStandardsRubrics.asp?ch=4#stnd4.

Nouwen, H. J. M. (September 1980). Do not worry, all things will be given. *Catholic Agitator.*

Office of Vocational and Educational Services for Individuals with Disabilities (VESID), the New York State Education Department. (2005). Regulations of the Commissioner of Education: Part 200—students with disabilities. Retrieved February 8, 2007, from http://www.vesid.nysed.gov/specialed/publications/lawsandregs/coverpage.htm.

Pearl, C. (2004). Laying the foundation for self-advocacy: Fourth graders with learning disabilities invite their peers into the resource room. *Teaching Exceptional Children, 36*(3), 44–49.

౮ 10

ETHICS, RESEARCH, AND REFLECTION
A Teaching Journey of the Heart

Gina A. Goble

It is not the answer that enlightens, but the question.

—Eugene Ionesco Decouvertes

Chapter Overview

- As a teacher researcher, the type of research you carry out is not the most important factor. What is far more important is to remember that there are children's lives at stake and they need to be protected and nourished by gentle, caring hearts.
- Teacher research can be exciting, invigorating, and refreshing to the teacher. It can rejuvenate your soul, and the process of reflection can revitalize your enthusiasm.

Inspirational Reflection

I chose to become a teacher because of educators in my past and current mentors who have inspired me and have taught me that teaching means more than the delivery of information. They all have one particular characteristic in common that sets them apart from the rest: all of them have shared pieces of their personal lives and have made connections that have broadened my awareness beyond the classroom. All of these teachers and mentors have made connections with their hearts. As educators, we are always trying to make cognitive connections to help our students understand, but to truly do so, to truly gain the trust and interest of our students, we need to put our hearts into our work. Our students need to feel that we are connected to them and that we care for them.

I have discovered that many, in the field of education, are connected to our hearts. Every day in the classroom, we make decisions based on curriculum, student learning needs and what goals we want to achieve with our students. But we do not do this blindly. We approach each decision using our "heart's eye" and our "ethical eye." With our "heart's eye," we decide how and if our students would benefit from the learning. We keep the students in mind and that is what we teach. Learning experiences are approached with compassion, and when we assess, we do so similarly.

Our "ethical eye" is just as critical. We are continuously making sure that what we present in the classroom is ethically sound. Our approaches, though creative, are grounded in research. Assessments we use are reliable and valid. We are careful to maintain a strong ethical stance as educators.

My first teaching experience, at twenty-one years of age, allowed me to be a loving, compassionate teacher, not having to concern myself with No Child Left Behind (NCLB), state test scores, and every punitive detail in my lesson plans. In fact, sixteen years ago, no child *was* left behind, at least not in my classroom or the classrooms of my colleagues. That experience allowed me to focus on the children and to teach from the heart. This is not to say that issues such as NCLB are unimportant, however; I learned that children are my purpose for waking up and going to school each day. Unfortunately, after I left that experience, it was not until twelve years later that I found myself working in a school where children were once again valued and *expected* to be put first. I was invited to teach at a pilot program and I was once again permitted to truly teach from the heart.

Three years ago, I was given the opportunity to work in the "Academy Project," a project school in an urban district in central New Jersey. This school was based on the following tenets: smaller class sizes, community and parental involvement, site-based decision making, and job-embedded professional development. It was the professional development aspect that required me to select a type of teacher research, carry it out during the year, and present my findings to our staff and administration at the conclusion of the year. The belief of this project was that, if all of the tenets were accomplished, an urban, at-risk school could be as successful as our suburban counterparts. For me, it was the opportunity of a lifetime. It was in doing research in that school that I learned ethics plays a very important role because our research subjects were primarily innocent Latino children who needed to be held with caring hands and compassionate hearts.

As my research model, I chose action research, not really knowing what I was up against. Nobody discussed ethics with us, and as I was new to the program, I was told to select a research topic and just begin. And so I did, but not without a struggle. I had no idea what to do or where to begin. In fact, at first,

I did not even know what action research was; I just knew that I loved to write and this school was going to give me the opportunity to write professionally. I knew I had to do something to get started, so I picked up some books and began to read. I needed to know what action research was all about and where to begin. As I read, I learned that first and foremost, research meant ethics, and ethics meant following moral principles and rules of conduct. Even though I knew about ethics, I was uncertain about how to apply it specifically in the classroom research environment.

Even though I had this new responsibility, my first task was to continue to provide a nurturing environment for my children as well as my colleagues (Hubbard & Power, 1999). I realized that this new venture was an opportunity for me to learn how to balance my teaching and classroom responsibilities with research embedded into my daily routine. Something else I learned almost immediately was that I needed a concrete, tangible baseline and continuous data from my students to record their progress. Without this important component I would not have anything to compare with my final data. I also knew that the data had to be genuine and in no way contrived. So I set out to find where my interests were the strongest, and thus I began my action research project, "The Pen Pal Project: Correspondence between Second Grade Students and Pre-Service Teachers." This is where I began my first journey of the heart.

Challenges Related to Ethical Decision Making

While doing my research, I came up against many hurdles. There were times when I questioned why I had transferred to this school. There were also times when I doubted the validity of my research and wondered how reliable my research tools were. Being new to action research, I constantly questioned myself, later learning that those questions were helpful. Every thought and question which presented itself was viewed through both the "heart's eye" and the "ethical eye." I needed a way to organize my thoughts and maintain my focus, and so I began to write everything down. By doing this, I was actually clarifying and narrowing my project. One of the easiest mistakes for a teacher researcher to make is to enter into too broad a research question. To make my teacher research possible, I needed to narrow down my interests to one specific idea. I found that the best way to do this was to write question after question until I reached the final question — the one question that I would be able to answer by applying a new technique.

I found many other minor challenges in the research I did, such as gaining parental support and approval as well as working the research into my classroom routine. One of the most frustrating hurdles was trying to meet with the other educators in my research group. They did not know my students as well as I did, and it posed a challenge as we tried to work together as a team, wanting to understand and respect each other's thoughts and ideas. Also, because they did not know my students well, they did not know the fundamentals of the research project (which was supposed to be a group effort), yet we were all contributors to this research project. However, I learned early on that if I was going to consider doing future research, I would encounter similar hurdles along my journey. To deal with this appropriately, I had to be patient and work with them to the best of my ability. I had to be ethical and willing to open myself to sharing my data with my colleagues because they *were* part of my action research group, even though they did not know my students as well as I did. For this reason, I had to reach inside myself and give all I could to our project because of my students. When they wanted to take shortcuts or make decisions that were not completely ethically sound, I had to speak up because it was my group of children who were the subjects of this project. At times I wanted to stand up and scream because of the frustration I felt, but instead I had to sigh, take a deep breath, and remind myself that this was an experience in learning how to work professionally with others as well as writing research. In the long run, I found that being professional and ethical with my colleagues was the best solution.

During the project, the most daunting of situations that I encountered had to do with administrative concerns and the need to answer a number of questions, both ethical and not, to help my research to continue moving forward. The children's progress in my project was not the primary focus of the administrators. Instead, they were concerned with how my research and its outcomes were going to make my school and my district look. They wanted responses to the following questions: How was it supporting NCLB? Which of the Core Curriculum Content Standards was I covering? How much of the school day was this going to consume? How was it going to improve test scores? And on, and on, and on! I have to admit that there were times when the questions made me question myself and the validity and reliability of my model. But it was in those moments when I realized that action research or, actually, any type of teacher research was fairly new and their questions were important to them and important for me to consider as I got deeper and deeper into the project. This was just another example of ethics. The administrators were acting ethically, in their role, as was I, in my role. Often, their questions were challenging to answer because I had not thought specifically about them, but in retrospect my children were involved in a learning process; we just stepped outside of the box to cover some of the standards. The administration would eventually see that. Quite honestly, the road became lonely at times, and the only way I could continue my project was to reach inside myself and remember that I was doing something to advance the education of my children. Deep inside, I knew that they were learning, but sometimes I needed to pay attention to exactly how much the students were gaining from their pen pal relationships in order to remind myself.

Ethical Teaching Strategies

In doing the research, I had to rely on specific strategies. I was working directly with a colleague who was a college professor to preservice teachers at a prestigious university. Before beginning, we set the plan, and we tried as hard as possible to maintain its integrity. Because I was working with an "outsider," I had to encourage my administrator that the outcomes were not going to be published with any "school name or district" and that my specific research project was one that could, if anything, only enhance student achievement. My second-grade students were corresponding biweekly with preservice teachers, and so they were writing on a regular basis. I had to convince them that the children were not, in any way, going to be harmed and that my research was going to be written to the highest standards, with the best consultants at hand. Because my students were involved in communicating with "strangers," I had to make sure that last names were not given and that personal information, such as their addresses and telephone numbers, was not revealed. This was yet another way in which ethics appeared in the research.

As the children got to know their pen pals through the letters, they wanted to share more information. After they wrote their letters I had to read over each letter to make sure personal information was not shared. In doing so, though, I did not alter them, because I did not want to affect the outcomes. This was another example of how important it was to evaluate the process using my "ethical eye" because it was their letters, in the original form, that were what I was interested in studying and using as a measurement tool throughout the process. While reading the letters, I looked to make sure that identifying information was not given out to their pen pals, and together each student and I looked to make sure that they answered the questions their pen pal asked, while asking their pen pals new questions. After exchanging a few letters, my students wanted to send pictures of themselves. This situation arose when their pen pals asked them to describe what they looked like. Again, because of ethical reasons, I had to go through administration and parents to gain permission to take and send photos. Because I had taken on this research and because I was working with children, everything had to be ethically sound.

As we continued through the year, my collection of data grew. I took photographs of the children as they received and read their letters. I started sitting back and observing them and jotting down their enthusiastic remarks and their desire to share their newly learned information about their pen pals. It was at that point in my research that I learned that my students had really connected and that their pen pal had become somebody real and special to them. It was harder and harder for them to wait for each new letter.

Each exchange of letters brought many new surprises to both my students and the preservice teachers. My second-grade students had developed writing skills beyond their grade level, which was noticeable in the depth of content in their letters as well as in their ability to construct letters that were full of exciting details about themselves and information they wanted to share with their pen pals. The preservice teachers were instructed to ask questions that would promote learning, such as asking them to name their favorite books or authors and identify which subjects they liked best at school. The children eagerly responded and filled one to three pages with answers to the questions and new questions for their pen pals. As the project progressed through the year, the letter writing became a homework assignment because the children were spending incredible amounts of time writing detail after detail to their newfound friends.

Like my colleague at the university, I found myself excited and astonished to see the growth of my children. We had successfully created a partnership between young children and preservice teachers, who expressed their interest in the youngsters who wrote letters to them. As my colleague and I compared notes, we both realized how touching this project was for all involved. She shared with me how her college students waited anxiously for the letters to arrive, and when she walked into class carrying a large yellow envelope, her students could not focus on the content of her instructional objectives until they had read their letters and shared the new information they learned from my students. Although the project was constructed as a research project for my program, the preservice students gained valuable lessons about second-language learners and the writing strategies and constructs of emergent readers and writers. In a survey given to the college students at the conclusion of the project, the general consensus was that the project was an experience they felt fortunate to have had.

Synthesis of Ethical Lessons Learned

Throughout the research, I learned that the children, although subjects, were not "guinea pigs." They were children filled with joy and enthusiasm, and it was in my best interest to remind myself of this fact daily. I made sure that, to the best of my knowledge, the information I used was true and accurate and the project that I selected was one that could benefit not only my students but at least one other educator in the field.

In the case of this action research project, it appeared to provide a positive learning experience for all involved. The college students gained valuable experiences as they read letters and responded to letters from my class. They deserve accolades for the ways in which they were able to engage and excite the second-grade children in wanting to read and write. Meanwhile, first written letters were compared with final letters, beginning DIBELS (Dynamic Indicator of Basic Early Literacy Skills) scores were compared with final DIBELS scores, and attitudes about reading and writing were also compared. All in all, my second-grade students scored 34 percent higher on the DIBELS than they were expected to at their grade level.

To sum up, I learned many important lessons as a teacher researcher. One of the most important things is that much of the finest research is disseminated from teacher educators and professional researchers who collect work diligently to stay abreast of what classroom teachers are facing today. However, some of the newer action research comes from teachers in the field who know their children, have great ideas, and also want to make a difference in the field of education.

Education has changed a lot in the seventeen years that I have been teaching. Teaching has become more challenging and it is important to stay on top of what is going on in the field. I have learned that one of the best ways to do so is by reading the current trends in research and continuing to apply these new strategies, when appropriate, in the classroom. As long as we approach every experience with ethically thought out ideas, we can continue to help our students be successful.

It also seems as if the teacher is becoming the new researcher in the field of education. We need to make our voices heard because what we do in the classroom has a long-lasting effect on the lives of our students. As I learned through this research project, action research is a new and exciting way to become more engaged in the process of teaching and learning. It can be time-consuming or tedious at times, but it is also an invigorating and exciting way to learn more and achieve more in the classroom environment.

Questions for Consideration

At the start of your research, create a reflective journal. Write down all of the questions you have and all of the ideas you wish to incorporate. Look at each question or thought through your "heart's eye" and then look at them again with an "ethical eye." Are you able to see a connection between the two? Write about that connection.

After selecting one research question, think about the various types of data that could be used to support your research. Write down these different types. Look at each type of data and write down how it will provide you with results that are both valid and reliable. If you need to, jot down the pros and cons of each type of data.

Supplementary Resources

Getting Started in Classroom Research: Dana, N. F., & Yendol-Silva, D. (2003). *The reflective educator's guide to classroom research: Learning to teach and teaching to learn through practitioner inquiry*. Thousand Oaks, CA: Corwin. This professional resource is a wonderful hands-on book for any teacher who is taking the first steps in the process of becoming a teacher researcher. It is full of ideas and answers to many of those ethical questions we have when we are just starting out. It also contains many questions that help us to reflect on our current teaching practices.

Exemplary Practices in Pen Pal Relationships: Berrill, D. P., & Gall, M. (2000). *Penpal programs in primary classrooms*. Ontario, Canada: Pembroke. This is an incredible resource for anyone who wants to have an involved pen pal relationship with another class or group of people. It provides the educator with sound ideas from what to expect from different ages of writers to how to assess your students' letter-writing abilities. It has great suggestions for books that could be used as read-alouds to introduce students to the ideas of becoming somebody's pen pal. It does an excellent job of modeling letters to pen pals as well as letters to parents explaining that their child will be participating in a pen pal exchange.

Integrating Ethics into the Classroom: Denenberg, D., & Roscoe, L. (2006). *50 American heroes every kid should meet*. Minneapolis, MN: Millbrook Press. This resource should be in every classroom. It takes children on an adventure through the lives of many important people, as it discusses their lives, accomplishments, and roles they played in the history of America. It is full of great quotes, unknown and interesting facts, and even people that some may not have considered as heroes. It is a book that provides our children with authentic heroes in a day and age when they need them more than ever, and it does so in a way that will intrigue them and encourage them to want to read more about the heroes in this book.

Reference

Hubbard, R. S., & Power, B. M. (1999). *Living the questions: A guide for teacher-researchers*. York, ME: Stenhouse.

◌◌ *11*

Journeying from Imposed Silence to Audacious Voice as a Teacher Researcher

Debra Dyer

Theories are stories and authors of theories are storytellers.

—*Nancy Rule Goldberger, 1996*

Chapter Overview

- Educational policy and practice crafted by those far removed from actual classrooms often requires silenced teacher technicians for classroom implementation.
- Teachers who conduct action research in their classrooms become the experts and theorists who craft the policy and practice that best suits their students' needs.
- Action research allows classroom teachers to use their silence and voice to transform classrooms into places of reflective practice and responsive and passionate teaching/learning committed to social justice.

Inspirational Reflection

In my thirty-two years as a public school teacher, I witnessed and was often a participant in the imposition of "scientifically based" research policy that had emanated from sterile contexts devoid of teacher and student voices. Teachers posed as voiceless conduits of policymakers' decisions, and children posed as voiceless receivers of decontextualized "stuff." The stories of the important stakeholders in education—the children, teachers, and families—were often muffled and rendered silent. However, through the use of action research, those closest to the data—the children, teachers, and families—can provide a rich, research corpus of data gathered from the narratives of their daily lives.

Narrative as a data-gathering method has been validated during the past few decades of social science, anthropological and philosophical research (Denzin & Lincoln, 2000). To understand people's perspectives, we must elicit their stories. Joan Didion (1979) states: "We tell ourselves stories in order to live. We live ... by the imposition of a narrative line upon disparate images, by the 'ideas' with which we have learned to freeze the shifting phantasmagoria which is our actual experience" (p. 11). By departing from conventional means of collecting and interpreting research to craft the narratives of our lives, we may create better ways to represent knowledge about educational practice (Florio-Ruane, 1991).

Autoethnography is one form of narrative that can be used effectively in action research. It is

> an autobiographical genre of writing and research that displays multiple layers of consciousness, connecting the personal to the cultural. Back and forth autoethnographers gaze, first through an ethnographic wide-angle lens, focusing outward on social and cultural aspects of their personal experience; then, they look inward, exposing a vulnerable self that is moved by and may move through, refract, and resist cultural interpretations. (Ellis & Bochner, 2000, p. 739)

The term "autoethnography" has been in use for over two decades, with Hayano (1979) usually being credited as the originator of the term. Hayano used the term in a more limited way than it is used today. In his definition, "autoethnography is a cultural-level study by anthropologists of their own people, in which the researcher is a full insider by virtue of being native, acquiring an intimate familiarity with the group, or achieving full membership in the group being studied" (p. 100). Antithetical to scientifically based research, which demands objectivity, generalization, and voiceless distance, action research honors the closeness and familiarity researchers enjoy as they peer through their data-gathering lens.

Through the use of teacher autoethnography, we can trace "the indirect ways that students and teachers mediate the outside of the official school curriculum through their multiple and changing experiences and constructions of self" (Ellsworth, 1997, p. 78). Ellis and Bochner describe autoethnography thus:

> Usually written in first-person voice, autoethnographic texts appear in a variety of forms—short stories, poetry, fiction, novels, photographic essays, personal essays, journals. ... In these texts, concrete actions, dialogue, emotion, embodiment ... are featured, appearing as relational and institutional stories affected by history, social structure, and culture. (2000, p. 739)

Personal stories, journals, and essays offer a different relationship between researcher, participant, and reader by providing a more collaborative, personal construction of meaning. In action research, autoethnography may be used to deconstruct events within a specific context, not necessarily to universalize theory and practice, but to achieve a coherent understanding of the past. In retelling the past, we expose our values, we articulate our perspective, and we seek meaning through the existence of our stories.

So often, teachers are viewed by educational policymakers as powerless technicians who are expected to use their voices solely to convey the thoughts of expert researchers. The silence imposed upon teachers constructs an institutional prison in which they are expected to teach children. However, the use of autoethnography in action research allows teachers to become bona fide experts in educational research, adding to the corpus of knowledge, providing the fortress in which teacher researchers use both strategic silence and expert voice.

Challenges Related to Ethical Decision Making— Silence As a Prison

In the 1986 work *Women's Ways of Knowing*, Belenky, Clinchy, Goldberger, and Tarule described *silence* as a position of "not knowing" and as a way women protect themselves and hide from dangerous authority. Silence was defined as the state of being unable to speak for fear of revealing one's lack of understanding, literally being unable to find words to communicate with others around one. For the authors of *Women's Ways of Knowing*, silence represents powerlessness and lack of control. However, Gallas (1998) notes that "silence as a personal position is a far safer place to maintain a sense of control over any situation, but silence is both a fortress and a prison" (p. 53).

In the early part of my teaching career—before I became an action researcher in my classroom—I silently accepted externally imposed policy and practice in my classroom. My silence was a debilitating condition that plagued me professionally and continues to afflict many classroom teachers who do not feel confident in their ability to collect and interpret data from their own classrooms. Much of that erosion of confidence that renders us silent and imprisoned in our classrooms is due to our relinquishment of our expert knowledge to those who are considered to be validated researchers. Teachers who view themselves more as silent technicians than skilled classroom researchers succumb to the overwhelming and misplaced authority of the official research community.

When we as teachers relinquish the control of research and data gathering to those in distant places—when we choose to delete the stories of our lives and our students—we are giving credence to the inappropriate practice that then is imposed in our classrooms. When we as teachers surrender our role as researchers, we are disempowered in our own classrooms and our professional acquiescence and silence become our prison.

When silence imprisons the classroom teacher, the authority of the policymakers fills the vacuum of the classroom and diminishes the presence of teacher authority in the life of the classroom. The scripted words of the curriculum are someone else's, and the teacher and students in their silence "believe that the source of self-knowledge is lodged in others—not in the self" (Belenky et al., 1986, p. 31). Time and again as a teacher technician, I silently and unquestioningly accepted imposed policy and program, becoming the conduit of someone else's theory and knowledge.

However, in assuming the role of an action researcher, we choose to become the educational experts, the data collectors and analyzers, the decision makers and policy creators in our classrooms as well as in our school communities. We choose to use our silence strategically as a defensive fortress in which to observe, collect data, reflect, and then to become outspoken in battling to retain authentic and appropriate educational practice. Through our expert knowledge as action researchers we can utilize our silence as well as our voices to both collect and tell the stories of our classroom communities. We can become the outspoken advocates for our students.

Ethical Teaching Strategies—Silence As a Fortress

In response to Belenky et al.'s (1986) work on silence, Aida Hurtado (1996) examined silence as a mechanism as a recursive theme in the writings of feminists of color from different ethnic/racial groups. Silence and the resulting outspokenness emphasize the concern for women of color developing their own voices. Hurtado (1996) contends that silence is one powerful strategy that women of color use with a specific goal in mind.

Tactical or strategic silence is used as a tool, particularly for those negotiating life in communities or workplaces where they are a minority or an outlier—culturally, racially, and socially. In utilizing strategic silence, a person may survey the environment, gather data, and sort out the data internally. Often, the purpose of this self-imposed silence is to watch how those in the dominant culture negotiate their behavior, reactions, and voice to then enable a safer entrée into that environment.

Through strategic silence, a woman of color learns by observing the workings of power in the dominant culture and then develops her authoritative voice by returning to her community to share what she has learned (Hurtado, 1989). Often that voice assumes what Hurtado called outspokenness. Outspokenness is the complementary strategy and can be used effectively, particularly when one knows exactly what one is saying and is not expected to have the knowledge to speak articulately. By using outspokenness, women of color can test their knowledge, practice their ideas, and sharpen their debating skills (Hurtado, 1996).

In my later years as a kindergarten teacher and action researcher, I made the walls of my classroom a fortress into which inappropriate practice for young children could not enter. In the public arena of my classroom this fortress also became a living, breathing data collection site in which I could as an ethnographer silently collect data, while writing as a way to find my "voice" as an academic (Elbow, 1973).

Unlike the silent teacher technician, who often loses her identity and sense of self when she allows external authority to speak for her, I chose silence as a very specific strategy (Hurtado, 1996). My tactic was to use the data, as I lived inside of my kindergarten fortress and viewed out of its peepholes, to better inform my teacher practice and as a standard against which I could continue to refine the pedagogy I crafted with my students.

My journey into action research began in 1995 when I assumed the role of a teacher researcher investigating the benefits or drawbacks of transitional classes in early childhood education. Through an awakening interest in educational policy and practice, I began to read, research, and experiment with action research in my classroom (although I did not know at the time it was called action research). I started with very simple questions that my students' behavior, dispositions, and difficulties would provoke. I would then follow the research protocol—asking a question, reading the research, designing a methodology for data collection, analyzing the data, instituting some type of change, and observing the implications. The result of this continuous reflective-researching disposition was to develop what I believe is a commitment to responsive teaching. It was fortuitous that in 2001 I was invited to co-teach a course on action research, and I later developed a university syllabus to teach it to prospective teachers.

During these years of transforming myself into an action researcher, I also transferred much of my inquiry approach into the pedagogy and curriculum of my kindergarten classroom. By allowing children to be researchers, I encouraged them to use both their strategic silence to observe and collect data and their confident, expert voices to explain the new knowledge they had created. My kindergarten students became articulate theorists, scientists, inventors, and creators.

I could never have predicted the transformation of my thinking in the past twelve years. I could never have envisaged my present dedication to teacher education that imagines the possibility of inspiring a new generation of passionate, reflective, and responsive teacher researchers who use their voices to articulate and loudly endorse policy and practice of which they are the expert researchers. But moving from a role of silenced teacher technician to strategically silent and outspoken teacher researcher has allowed me to dream the impossible for the future in teacher education.

Synthesis of Ethical Lessons Learned — Creating Passionate, Reflective, Responsive Teachers Committed to Social Justice

The growth of passionate, reflective, responsive educators committed to social justice cannot be fostered until educators also assume a pragmatic stance toward national, state, and local policy. Teacher education must prepare teachers for the reality of policy constraints that will continue to be imposed on public schools. Future teachers will constantly be buffeted by the ebb and flow of policy and pedagogy: "endless mandates and directives from faceless bureaucrats ... dictating frequently absurd practices" (Cohn & Kottkamp, 1993, p. 222). Teachers as caring, passionate, reflective partners in learning with their students, collaboratively creating new theory and committed to social justice, can flourish within the walls of their classrooms.

Passionate Teachers

Teaching, though identified as a profession like medicine or law, is a unique profession in that it involves trust, respect, and relationships. Passion for learning, love for children, and a desire to share one's passion for learning with those we love are the very core of teaching. However, this is not a sentimental love that teachers have for their students, but a "fundamental belief in the lives and minds of students ... a blend of confidence, faith, and admiration for students and appreciation for the strengths they bring with them" (Nieto, 2003, pp. 37–38).

Care in teaching is demonstrated by truly accepting students and making them feel that they belong to a community respectful of their diverse cultural and language backgrounds. Caring is a solid belief in individual capabilities of students to learn. Passion for teaching is a persistent belief in students and patience for the gradual transference of genuine teacher confidence in the students' abilities to each student in the form of personal self-confidence (Nieto, 2003).

To become a passionate teacher

> is to be someone in love with the field of knowledge, deeply stirred by issues and ideas that challenge our world, drawn to the dilemmas and potentials of the young people

who come into class each day—or captivated by all of these. (Fried, 1995, p. 1)

Cohn and Kottkamp (1993) write that the purpose of the passionate teacher has always been to help students grow academically and as whole human beings. Passion in teaching requires that teachers do not assume the characteristic of raw material being pressed into shape by educational policy in order to then do the same to their students. Instead, passionate teachers are called to find their voice, are fueled by a genuine anger at their silencing and the silencing of students, and are motivated by a deep caring for their students.

Reflective Researchers

In teacher education, we endeavor to graduate reflective teachers who "play active roles in formulating the purposes and ends of their work ... teachers who play leadership roles in curriculum development and school reform" (Zeichner, Melnick, & Gomez, 1996, p. 199). The concept of the reflective teacher acknowledges the wealth of expertise that resides in the practices of teachers, what Schön (1983) has called "knowledge-in-action." Reflecting on and reconstructing these daily interactions with children through talking and writing provides rich data through which a teacher can then shape her or his pedagogy and practice.

Schön (1983) speaks of the reflective practitioner as a teacher who, over a longer period of time rather than minute by minute, is trying to make sense of phenomena in the classroom and

> reflects on the understandings which have been implicit in his action, understandings which he surfaces, criticizes, restructures, and embodies in further action. It is this entire process of reflection-in-action which is central to the "art" by which practitioners sometimes deal well with situations of uncertainty, instability, uniqueness, and value conflict. (p. 50)

This teacher disposition of reflection catalyzes the process of understanding and improving one's own teaching, starting from reflection on one's own experience. Teachers who believe in their students, who value the experiences their students bring to the classroom, who listen to the dialogue of the classroom, and who will allow students to "sit and listen as well as to talk and to think, emphasize that the process of 'coming to know' is as valuable as knowing the 'right answer'" (Fu & Stremmel, 1999, p. 162). This is the type of reflective teachers we want in our classrooms.

Reflective teachers then assume the role of reflective teacher researchers who enter into modes of inquiry very different from the model of institutionalized research. "The practitioner does not function here as a mere user of the researcher's product. ... He reveals the ways of thinking that he brings to his practice, and draws on reflective research as an aid to his own reflection-in-action" (Schön, 1983, p. 323).

The reflective practitioner takes time out to become a reflective researcher, moving in and out of research and practice through the use of action research. Action research is a vehicle of inquiry that informs the teacher about policy, practice, and their translation into the local site of the classroom.

Action research is

> any systematic inquiry conducted by teacher researchers, principals, school counsel-
> ors, or other stakeholders in the teaching/learning environment, to gather informa-
> tion about the ways that their particular schools operate, how they teach, and how
> well their students learn. This information is gathered with the goal of gaining insight,
> developing reflective practice, effecting positive changes in the school environment
> (and on educational practices in general), and improving student outcomes and the
> lives of those involved. (Mills, 2000, p. 6)

Action research creates opportunities for all involved to improve the lives of children, by looking critically at what we do in our classrooms, and the effects of what we do on our students. Action research engenders in teachers a disposition of the lifelong learner, which models to their students how knowledge is created (Mills, 2000).

In teacher education, helping our teachers become more reflective is one of the major goals. In becoming a reflective teacher, one looks locally at one's teaching so that one can improve and enhance it, examine the dynamics of the classroom, think about student interactions, and either validate or challenge one's practice. At a more global level, action research provides the opportunity for teachers to become reflective about educational research, theoretical knowledge, educational equity and policy, and the translation of these entities into daily life in their classroom practice.

Commitment and action are inherent in action research. Action research is relevant because it is situated in the uniqueness of the individual classroom context. Action research gives teachers access, with a specific focus, to the most recent research on a topic and then allows the teacher to use that research as a jumping-off point to inform their own data collection. "Action research gives teacher-researchers the opportunity to embrace a problem-solving philosophy as an integral part of the culture of their schools ... and to challenge the intractability of educational reform by making action research a part of the system" (Mills, 2000, pp. 14–15).

Responsive Teachers

Responsive teaching emphasizes collaboration and active participation by both partners in learning and teaching. It is a delicate balance of strategy (both questioning and explanation) where the teacher needs to possess a knowledge of each child's level of functioning, social and cultural schema, and a sense of when to intervene and when to step back to allow students to make self-discoveries (Fu & Stremmel, 1999). By drawing on a variety of teaching methods—direct instruction, inquiry-based, small-group work, large-group introduction and debriefing, reciprocal teaching, literature circles, partnered investigation—responsive teaching offers the best means of recognizing and accommodating the perspectives, values, and experiences of students from diverse cultures (Rogoff & Wertsch, 1984).

Although teachers are sincere in being responsive and reaching out to all their students, it sometimes is impossible when teachers do not know much about the lives of the students they teach. One of the first steps teachers must take in creating a culturally responsive and relevant learning environment is to engage in reflective self-analysis, to examine their attitudes toward different ethnic, racial, social class, and gender groups (Delpit, 1995). This journey begins with teachers' self-reflection and then their examination of the racism, biased attitudes, and resulting behaviors that are structured into schools and the wider society.

Responsive teachers build relationships with their students, fostering mutual respect and trusting collaboration for learning. Thoughtful communication is an imperative for building the necessary trust, and teacher words have a great impact (Nieto, 2003). Being a responsive teacher is a holistic attitude that pervades the academic, social, and emotional persona of a teacher and is reflected in her or his words as well as in her or his behavior.

Through a dedication to responsive teaching, teachers provide intellectual challenges by teaching to high standards and by communicating to their students confidence in student competence to meet and exceed those high standards (Ladson-Billings, 1994). The rigor of meeting high standards often requires the teacher to provide instructional scaffolding by encouraging students to build upon their own unique knowledge, skills, and experience to then move into more difficult knowledge and skills.

Increasing the continuity between students' home experiences and the school environment is particularly crucial to the success of children from diverse cultures and social classes. For children to construct a confident self-identity, the responsive teacher must acknowledge and build on cultural differences, at the same time preparing children to live successfully in both the world of the dominant culture and their home culture (Delpit, 1995).

Rethinking teacher education is necessary to promote the growth of responsive teachers. Nieto (2003) stresses the importance of teacher education that goes beyond an emphasis on strategies and techniques for teaching and becomes "a way of thinking about learning, and of one's students, and of what will be most useful for them … all teachers need to know more about the students they teach" (p. 125).

Educators Committed to Social Justice

Teachers entering the profession are often motivated by sensitivity to the social injustice that is perpetuated in public schools and society at large, and are dedicated to eradicating it and replacing it with social justice. A life of service exemplified by a commitment to the ideals of democracy, fair play, and equality is common among teachers (Nieto, 2003). Poverty and racism, manifested in the lack of school resources, unequal funding for students' education, and unqualified teachers, catalyzes the anger in social justice–committed teachers. For these teachers, teaching demonstrates their commitment to democracy (hooks, 1994).

In the struggle for equal education, teachers who demonstrate a commitment to social justice interrogate the institutional and structural inequality of public schooling. Often, this happens in small groups of like-minded teachers in a school or district who join together to share their anger, hopes, beliefs, and assumptions about students and teaching. Out of this grassroots assembly, teacher research groups, political action coalitions, and intellectual communities are born.

The zeal for intellectual excellence combined with a belief in social justice can be used for the betterment of schools and, as a curriculum, can provide students with an apprenticeship in critical inquiry of democracy. It is about those modest as well as extravagant actions we do as teachers committed to social justice for our students and society at large (Freire, 1970). It is also about modeling for our students democracy as a way of life, "a life of social progress and reform" (Dewey, 1940, p. 337).

By silently listening, we learn from one another. By actively listening, we free the voices of those whose silence is reflective of their inability to make their voices heard, who have internalized a learned silence, or who believe their voices are not important. Through action research, teachers may unleash their sanctioned silence, use their strategic silence to collect and analyze data, and then use the stories of their classrooms as the audacious researcher voice advocating reflection, responsiveness, passion, and commitment to equity.

Questions for Consideration

It took almost three decades for me to journey from imposed silence as a teach-er technician to gaining an audacious voice as a teacher researcher. How can we (teacher educators, administrators, mentors) support young educators in valuing and conducting action research in their classrooms?

Reflect on the current policy of NCLB and all its mandates. In what ways do classroom teachers and school administrators negotiate the ethical divide of authoritative requirements and individual classroom needs?

Supplementary Resources

Longevity in Teaching: Nieto, S. (2003). *What keeps teachers going?* New York: Teachers College Press. This thoughtful book uses data collected from class-room teachers to project the voice of passionate, reflective, and responsive teachers. Teachers provide advice in how to overcome the challenges relating to teacher longevity and guide us on a lifelong journey as powerful, effective classroom teachers.

Responsive Teaching in Classrooms Committed to Social Justice: Wink, J. (2000). *Critical pedagogy: Notes from the real world.* New York: Addison-Wesley Longman. This powerful analysis of the complex rhetoric of critical pedagogy argues that through the investigation of critical pedagogy, a broader and deeper perspective on teaching and learning in both the classroom and the community may be achieved. This book strongly encourages teachers to adapt teaching beliefs and strategies continuously to meet the needs of today's classrooms.

Passionate Teaching: Wink, J., & Wink, D. (2004). *Teaching passionately: What's love got to do with it?* Boston: Pearson. This book is an exploration of so-cial foundations from the theoretical, collaborative, and political perspectives. It asks: What is the place of love and passion in teaching and learning? In this age of mandated assessment and standards-based curricula, what can each teacher do to maintain the joy of learning and teaching?

References

Belenky, M., Clinchy, B., Goldberger, N., & Tarule, J. (1986). *Women's ways of knowing: The development of self, voice, and mind.* New York: Basic Books.

Cohn, M. M., & Kottkamp, R. B. (1993). *Teachers: The missing voice in education.* Albany, NY: New York State University Press.

Delpit, L. (1995). *Other people's children: Cultural conflict in the classroom.* New York:

New Press.

Denzin, N., & Lincoln, Y. (2000). *Handbook of qualitative research* (2nd ed.). Thousand Oaks, CA: Sage.

Dewey, J. (1940). *Education today.* New York: Putnam.

Didion, J. (1979). *The white album.* New York: Simon & Schuster.

Elbow, P. (1973). *Writing without teachers.* London: Oxford University Press.

Ellis, C., & Bochner, A. (2000). Autoethnography, personal narrative, and reflexivity. In N. Denzin & Y. Lincoln (Eds.), *Handbook of qualitative research* (2nd ed.) (pp. 550–562). Thousand Oaks, CA: Sage.

Ellsworth, E. (1997). *Teaching positions: Difference, pedagogy, and the power of address.* New York: Teachers College Press.

Florio-Ruane, S. (1991). Conversation and narrative in collaborative research. In C. Witherill & N. Noddings (Eds.), *Stories lives tell: Narrative and dialogue in education* (pp. 234–256). New York: Teachers College Press.

Freire, P. (1970). *Pedagogy of the oppressed.* New York: Seabury Press.

Fried, R. L. (1995). *The passionate teacher: A practical guide.* Boston: Beacon Press.

Fu, V., & Stremmel, A. (1999). *Affirming diversity through democratic conversations.* Upper Saddle River, NJ: Prentice Hall.

Gallas, K. (1998). *Sometimes I can be anything: Power, gender, and identity in a primary classroom.* New York: Teachers College Press.

Hayano, D. (1979). Autoethnography: Paradigms, problems, and perspectives. *Human Organization, 38,* 113–120.

hooks, b. (1994). *Teaching to transgress: Education as the practice of freedom.* New York: Routledge.

Hurtado, A. (1989). Reflections on white feminism: A perspective from a woman of color. In S. Chan (Ed.), *Social and gender boundaries in the United States* (pp. 155–186). Lewiston, ME: Edwin Mellon Press.

———. (1996). Strategic suspensions: Feminists of color theorize the production of knowledge. In N. Goldberger, J. Tarule, B. Clinchy, & M. Belenky (Eds.), *Knowledge, difference, and power* (pp. 372–392). New York: Basic Books.

Ladson-Billings, G. (1994). *The dreamkeepers: Successful teachers of African American children.* San Francisco: Jossey-Bass.

Mills, G. E. (2000). *Action research.* Upper Saddle River, NJ: Prentice Hall.

Nieto, S. (2003). *What keeps teachers going?* New York: Teachers College Press.

Rogoff, B., & Wertsch, J. (Eds.). (1984). *Children's learning in the "zone of proximal development."* San Francisco: Jossey-Bass.

Schön, D. A. (1983). *The reflective practitioner: How professionals think in action.* New York: Basic Books.

Zeichner, K., Melnick, S., & Gomez, M. (1996). *Currents of reform in preservice teacher education.* New York: Teachers College Press.

ca 12

THE IVORY TOWER IN THE BLACKBOARD JUNGLE
Striving for Coexistence

Katherine A. Dougherty Stahl

What truly marks an open-minded person is the willingness to follow where evidence leads. The open-minded person is willing to defer to impartial investigations rather than to his own predilections. … Scientific method is attunement to the world, not to ourselves.

—Adler, 1998, p. 44

Chapter Overview

Three years ago, I left the elementary classroom and accepted a university position as a teacher educator and researcher. In this chapter, I describe some of my experiences as I struggle to claim my new identity and to define my own ethical standards in this new role. I focus my attention on the following two questions that I have been grappling with as a newcomer to academia:

- What does it mean to be an ethical teacher educator?
- What does it mean to be an ethical educational researcher?

Inspirational Reflection

A Ph.D. graduate who specialized in secondary literacy education accepts a literacy position in a middle school. Within six weeks, he quits. The demands of the position and the curriculum requirements are inconsistent with his epistemology.

A middle school teacher asks a professor how the theoretical ideas that she is discussing might be applied in his middle school classroom. The in-service teacher works in a high-poverty school with poor achievement that is under scrutiny for maintaining progress toward the goals of No Child Left Behind (NCLB). The professor responds negatively to NCLB policies and their consequences, but she does not ever address how theoretically sound instructional strategies can be adapted to troubled settings.

A Ph.D. student is working in two elementary classrooms on a formative, pilot study. After several weeks, one of the experienced teachers states reservations about the practicality of one aspect of the study and invites the researcher to work with one of the small groups to get an insider's perspective on what is not working. The researcher minimizes the value of her input and ends the conversation by adding, "I don't need to become a grain of salt, to understand the chemical characteristics of sodium chloride." This Ph.D. student is a career changer who has never taught in a classroom but made a midlife decision that he wanted to make a difference in the world by contributing to school improvement.

These three vignettes are descriptions of situations that I observed during my doctoral program or in my first two years in academia. To me, they are demonstrations of the chasm between the realities of the classroom and the sterilized world of academia. This lack of connection has been the largest disillusionment and disappointment in my career shift. As someone who spent twenty-six years in elementary and middle school classrooms before entering academia, I am finding that my perspective is often quite different from that of my colleagues in schools of education, who tend to have little or no actual teaching experience outside the university classroom. These differences become exemplified in both my instruction and my research.

In this chapter, I hope to share the challenges that I have faced in trying to find a home in an ivory tower while staying situated in the realities of the blackboard jungle. In education, there is an ongoing tension between maintaining a status quo that does not serve all learners because "that won't work in our school" and the academic ivory tower's idealistic view of how things ought to be. Given the knowledge that researchers have acquired about effective practice, it seems unethical that so many students are not receiving instruction that meets their needs. Alternatively, the purity of in-depth study in one specific area is the luxury of researchers without the need to balance the complexities found within every school and classroom. Is it realistic or even ethical to expect teachers to superimpose these isolated kernels of knowledge on their ecological system? Despite the relationship between schools and educational research, these are often two very different worlds. During the last three years, it has been a challenge for me to traverse between these two worlds. Is it possible or desirable to build and sustain an ivory tower within the blackboard jungle?

Challenges Related to Ethical Decision Making

Preparing teachers to meet the literacy needs of a diverse group of learners is an ethical responsibility of schools of education. Research agrees that effective reading teachers are "knowledgeable, strategic, adaptive, responsive and reflective" (Hoffman et al., 2003, p. 1). However, schools of education face the challenge of providing the learning opportunities, resources, and time that will facilitate the acquisition of these competencies.

One group of senior preservice teachers in their first literacy course told me that I was teaching incorrectly. In my introductory literacy course, each class period consisted of both small-group and whole-group activities. Application of class learning occurred in a supervised field placement. However, whole-group instruction during our first month together often took the form of lectures to introduce or clarify theories and literacy vocabulary and to review general literacy concepts from their reading (such as the difference between phonological awareness and phonics) that were entirely new and unfamiliar to them. Throughout the semester, a student or I modeled an instructional or assessment technique during a portion of the whole-class instructional time. In addition to a field-based student case study and six literacy lessons, there was also a mid-term examination on literacy basics and situational application of the course content. The students were outraged at this level of specificity and accountability. They had been taught or had the impression from the other methods classes that *all* instruction should be inquiry-based, hands-on, and conducted in small, student-led discussion groups. Although these students were in a highly ranked, nationally respected educational program, they were more accustomed to being evaluated on the basis of personal reflection papers and group inquiry projects. Attitudes shifted in early November as they assumed increasing responsibility for literacy instruction in their field placements. As their teaching responsibilities increased, their appreciation for specific reading content knowledge and specific instructional teaching procedures increased.

These students entered their senior year and field placements with a great deal of experience reflecting and pontificating on classroom observations. Multiple methods classes had promoted an inquiry approach to the exclusion of other theoretical models. The students had been saturated with the importance of taking a sociocultural perspective. However, specific teaching strategies for situating content knowledge within a sociocultural perspective received less attention. So although our students could articulate a theory of learning, the melding of this theory with its practical application in ways that would enable them to meet the needs of a diverse population tended to be a missing piece.

I was a little surprised to find so many commonalities among novice teachers as I moved from a state institution in the Midwest to a private institution in a northeastern urban setting. Without exception, novice teachers advocate a sociocultural perspective and give credence to Garner's theory of multiple intelligences (1983/1993) for instructional planning. In my graduate courses, the certified teachers from a wide range of undergraduate teacher preparation programs typically seem knowledgeable about graphic organizers and KWL charts. Their schema for comprehension instruction typically consists of activating prior knowledge, taking a picture walk, or generating predictions, followed by various forms of reader response such as reader's theater, quick writes, journals, and artistic responses. They advocate a discussion of text that incorporates text–self, text–world, and text–text connections. However, I am surprised by the consistent voids in long-standing research-based practices. Cognitive strategy instruction, reciprocal teaching, vocabulary instruction, and, surprisingly, general principles of phonics instruction are typically unfamiliar to the newly certified teachers in my graduate-level classes. Differentiated small-group reading instruction also seems to be a missing piece. Round-robin reading and whole-group instruction still prevail. Without a bank of content knowledge and teaching strategies, the teachers are unable to be true to their theoretical ideals while being adaptive and responsive to their students' needs.

Although they can often define critical literacy, the novice teachers that I work with lack the confidence and the knowledge to critique either educational research in peer-reviewed publications or administrative policies that affect them and their students on a daily basis. They are intimidated by the text genre called the research article. As a result, they spend their days following district mandates, scripts, and pacing charts based on "scientific evidence." In the evenings, they come to graduate school and listen to diatribes about the harm of such policies and the research that led to the policies. However, there does not seem to be a space where they are guided to become critical consumers of research in ways that will serve their needs as they strive to find ways to help their students and to become the literacy leaders in their schools.

In my own education, I was lucky enough to be taught by two professors who exposed their students to a wide range of literacy research. They prodded thinking by questioning their students and the information in the articles that we read. In essence, they performed think-alouds that modeled the scientific process and the process of evaluating literacy research. I was impressed by the humility and fair-handedness these experts showed in addressing a wide range of literacy topics. They exemplified Adler's description of open-mindedness. The desire for a scholarly open-mindedness was instilled in me by their example. I do not think that I am alone in finding it difficult to extend my world beyond my own predilections for conversation with like-minded colleagues and research that supports my comfortable beliefs. However, my two professors were models of the scholar that I am striving to become.

My late husband was a wonderful research mentor (see Stahl, 2005; Stahl & McKenna, 2006). He emphasized that the purpose of research is to improve classroom reading instruction and children's reading achievement. Steve spent a great deal of time in classrooms, and he was the hands-on director of the University of Georgia Reading Clinic. As a result, he advocated research that was practical for teachers dealing with the realities of classroom life and that focused on helping students. When I was writing my dissertation, he tried to simplify things for me by asking, "What is the story that your research results tell? Just tell the story." He did not see an obscure, academic writing style as a sign of intellect. Although he never oversimplified the complexity of the reading process, he believed that the best writing made the intricacies comprehensible to the reading audience. As a classroom teacher (even before meeting him), I loved his research because he asked relevant, important questions and his clear writing style enabled me to make sense of his results and implications for my practice.

In a recent keynote speech, Pearson (2006) discussed the tension between educational research that improves our body of knowledge and research that improves classroom practice. He addressed the differences between basic research performed in a laboratory setting to help us know more and applied research performed in classrooms to make things better. "Some of us pretended that there were feedback loops from practice to both applied research and basic research and from applied to basic, but the truth is that the model was decidedly linear." So although both kinds of research clearly have an important function and both kinds of research are related to instruction, the pretension that Pearson refers to is where we face the danger of becoming unethical.

Ethical Teaching Strategies

The International Reading Association (IRA) has established a professional hierarchy of standards for paraprofessionals, certified teachers, and reading specialists (Task Force of the Professional Standards and Ethics Committee of the International Reading Association, 2004). Additionally, the IRA initiated and published a report from the National Commission on Excellence in Elementary Teacher Preparation for Reading Instruction, whose mission was to determine the program characteristics of effective reading teacher preparation and the impact of that preparation on both the graduates and their students (Hoffman et al., 2003). Together these documents provide some guidance on how schools of education might meet their ethical obligation to prepare teachers for the demands of literacy classrooms with students who have a wide range of needs.

The National Commission on Excellence in Elementary Teacher Preparation for Reading Instruction conducted a three-year study to identify characteristics of effective teaching programs and to investigate the outcomes of these
programs in terms of the classroom practices of their graduates and the reading
achievement of their students (Hoffman et al., 2003). They concluded that the
content of effective teacher preparation programs extensively covered the five
pillars of the National Reading Panel Report (phonological awareness, phonics, fluency, vocabulary, and comprehension), the assessment of these areas,
and the organization and management of literacy instruction across the grade
levels (National Institute of Child Health and Human Development, 2000).
The commission identified seven other critical features in the establishment
of a comprehensive, integrated teacher education program. Those additional
features are (1) an extensive, quality *apprenticeship* with excellent models; (2) a
cohesive program *vision;* (3) intellectual, financial, and professional *resources;* (4)
personalized teaching; (5) a sense of informed *autonomy* that instills the belief that
the needs of students, not bureaucracy, come first; (6) an active learning *community;* and (7) ongoing *assessment* of the students, the graduates, the program,
and the faculty.

This is a large order. However, as a researcher who also teaches in a school
of education it means that I have a moral obligation that extends beyond my
own research and personal areas of intellectual interest. Certainly, I should use
my own voice to bring my expertise and my passions to the students I teach.
However, in the role of teacher educator I need to keep an eye on the bigger
picture. I have an obligation to prepare teachers for the realities of the classroom in ways that are supported by a *wide* body of research. Working as a team
member to develop and implement a comprehensive, cohesive teacher education program, integrating theory and research-based teaching techniques, and
encouraging autonomy by teaching my students how to be critical consumers
of a range of educational research are what I consider to be the ethical responsibilities of the ivory tower to those who face the daily challenges of the
blackboard jungle.

I was disturbed on multiple levels by a comment made by a novice teacher
on my most recent course evaluations. "While I can appreciate the different
perspective, it was hard to take a course seriously that was based on the NRP
findings when all other professors that I had in this program have discredited
or seriously cast doubt." This confirmed that evidence-based research practices were not included in this student's undergraduate training. In her current
program, quantitative work and commissioned work, including work commissioned by the IRA, was being devalued rather than explored and evaluated.
Most disturbing was that she was allowing others with different purposes to
inform her decisions about research that she did not read. I had failed in my

ethical responsibility to give this teacher the essential tools that she needs to think independently about what might work best for the children she teaches.

> Interestingly, in these times when many are concerned about teacher autonomy, there is nothing that has greater potential for making teachers autonomous scholars than a knowledge of the scientific process and the ability to evaluate scientific evidence—that is, to be independent evaluators of knowledge claims. Such skills not only provide the best protection against gurus and fads, but they provide other benefits as well. They provide teachers with tools to win intellectual battles with (often misinformed) principals, school boards, parents, school psychologists, and other ancillary supervisors and personnel that attempt to dictate teacher practice. (Stanovich & Stanovich, 2006, p. 40)

The ethical standards established by the American Educational Research Association (AERA, 2004) can provide a framework for mediating the divide between classroom realities and the ivory tower. These standards address researchers' responsibilities to the field and their responsibilities to research populations, educational institutions, and the public. Both the preamble and the standards address responsibilities to the field that mirror the ethical obligations to our teacher education students. The preamble to the list of ethical standards states that researchers have a responsibility to be kept "well informed in both their own and competing paradigms where those are relevant to their research." The ability to engage in the peer-review process with intellectual honesty and respect is essential to the process of advancing scientific knowledge. Even quantitative researchers recognize the subjective aspects of their methodology. However, it is the checks-and-balances process of peer review, tests of replication, and the principles of converging evidence that enable us to move the field forward. Paradigm differences have the potential to provide the highest standard of critical analysis when approached with informed respect. This level of cross-checking is essential before we can make recommendations to our consumers, policymakers, and teachers (Stanovich & Stanovich, 2003).

Ethical Standard seven states:

> Educational researchers' reports to the public should be written straightforwardly to communicate the practical significance for policy, including limits in effectiveness and in generalizability to situations, problems, and contexts. In writing for or communicating with non-researchers, educational researchers must take care not to misrepresent the practical or policy implications of their research or the research of others. (AERA, 2004)

Basic research, applied research, and pedagogical research each fulfill important functions as we strive to expand the knowledge base in our field. However, in reporting our findings it is important for us to state clearly the boundaries of generalization and limitations of our research findings. Trust in our academic community and in paradigms that differ from our own can give us the freedom honestly to express the boundaries of our own research. Being part of a community means we do not need to do it all, nor do we need to have all the answers. Having a working knowledge of research that may differ from our own enables us to situate our work within the field and within the complexities that define school ecosystems. Masking the limitations does a disservice to our knowledge base, but it also damages the credibility of "research-based education" as teachers, administrators, and policymakers attempt to adapt our findings to ill-matched purposes or contexts.

Masking limitations occurs on a larger, more dangerous scale when we allow selected research to become privileged and used to vocationalize teachers (Pearson, 2006). When selected research informs educational policy in the form of scripts and pacing guides, teachers are discouraged from engaging in their own scientific thinking and critical analysis of the research. In essence, teacher professionalism and responsibility are abdicated.

Synthesis of Ethical Lessons Learned

Writing this chapter felt like a healthy stretch. As with all writing, this process enabled me to think in a more reflective way about the events of the last few years and personal future directions. I am in the right place for this stage of my career. It is fulfilling to research questions that emerged from my teaching. The promise of finding answers that have the potential to help more than the twenty-five students in my classroom is inspiring for me. I am excited to be actively involved in restructuring the language and literacy program in the Steinhardt School of Education. Many of the ideas in this chapter have been part of the conversations that I have had with my current colleagues as we engage in reshaping our program better to meet the needs of our teacher education students.

However, I have never written a public narrative. I have never written publicly about anything but literacy—certainly not ethics. Six pages into this essay I was ridden with anxiety surrounding this inexperience. Was I on the right track or was my writing too personal? How I wished that I could share my ideas with Steve. For eight years, one of the gifts of living with my husband, my friend, my mentor, and, finally, my colleague was the twenty-four-hour opportunity to exchange ideas and continue to expand my thinking about literacy, learning, food, music, and life. Living with Steve made me a better teacher. I could not read converging scientific evidence at home and do something different during the day with any sense of moral consciousness. On many occasions, I invited Steve to observe in my classroom when a technique didn't seem to be working or when what I was doing didn't seem to be helping a particular child. Time and again, viewing my classroom through the lens of a researcher provided insights that enabled me to adjust my instruction in ways that always benefited my students. Similarly, Steve asked for my opinions on his research and manuscripts. In our union, teaching and research informed each other. The coexistence improved the quality of the teaching and the research.

If we wish to improve the quality of teaching and research on a larger scale, coexistence on a larger scale is essential. The ivory tower must be situated in the blackboard jungle so that researchers don't lose sight of the complexity and the realities that teachers face in a school ecosystem. However, the tower enables researchers to have the broader view that is not always visible to the teacher immersed in the quotidian details and distractions of the classroom. Coexistence also ensures confrontation, communication, responsibility, and accountability to each other. These elements will enable us to meet the greater ethical responsibility that we each have to improve the education of our students.

Questions for Consideration

Reflect on a time when a district mandate required you to do something instructionally that you opposed. What is your ethical responsibility when a mandate does not seem to be in the best interests of the students or teachers who will be affected?

Reflect on your recent professional reading. Was it a peer-reviewed journal? How did it expand your thinking and what actions did you take as a result?

Supplementary Resources

Stanovich, K. E., & Stanovich, P. J. (2006). Fostering the scientific study of reading instruction by example. In K. A. D. Stahl & M. C. McKenna (Eds.), *Reading research at work: Foundations of effective practice* (pp. 36–44). New York: Guilford Press. Excerpt follows:

> For example, it is possible for teachers—in the most professional manner—to confront principals, learning disabilities specialists, and inservice gurus with the appropriate questions:
> "Has the evidence for this treatment been published in peer-reviewed scientific journals?" "If so, in what journals, so that I may provide the involved teachers with reprints of the studies?"
> "Have the studies that have been done on this treatment been more than case studies?" "Have they involved some type of control group?"
> "Is the proposed mechanism by which this treatment works consistent with the thirty-year consensus in the voluminous literature on the determinants of reading disabil-

ity?" "Have the results been replicated by independent researchers?" These are basic questions, and they can be used by informed teachers to great effect. (Stanovich & Stanovich, 2006, p. 40)

Stanovich, P. J., & Stanovich, K. E. (2003). *Using research and reason in education: How teachers can use scientifically based research to make curricular and instructional decisions.* Portsmouth, NH: National Institute for Literacy.

Task Force of the Professional Standards and Ethics Committee of the International Reading Association. (2004). *Standards for reading professionals—Revised 2003.* Retrieved February 11, 2006, from http://www.reading.org/resources/issues/reports/professional_standards.html.

References

Adler, J. E. (January 1998). Open minds and the argument from ignorance. *Skeptical Inquirer, 22*(1), 41–44.

American Educational Research Association. (2004). *Ethical standards.* Retrieved January 18, 2007, from http://www.aera.net/aboutaera/?id=173.

Gardner, Howard (1983; 1993). *Frames of mind: The theory of multiple intelligences.* New York: Basic Books.

Hoffman, J. V., Roller, C. M., Maloch, B., Sailors, M., Beretvas, N., & the National Commission on Excellence in Elementary Teacher Preparation for Reading Instruction. (2003). *Prepared to make a difference: Final report of the National Commission on Excellence in Elementary Teacher Preparation for Reading Instruction.* Newark, DE: The International Reading Association.

National Institute of Child Health and Human Development. (2000). *Report of the National Reading Panel. Teaching children to read: An evidence-based assessment of the scientific research literature on reading and its implications for reading instruction* (NIH Publication No. 00-4769). Washington, DC: U.S. Government Printing Office. Available from http://www.nationalreadingpanel.org.

Pearson, P. D. (November 2006). An historical analysis of the impact of educational research on practice: Reading as an illustrative case. Paper presented at the annual meeting of the National Reading Conference, Los Angeles, CA.

Stahl, K. A. D. (2005). Improving the asphalt of reading instruction: A tribute to the work of Steven Stahl. *The Reading Teacher, 59*, 184–192.

Stahl, K. A. D., & McKenna, M. C. (Eds.). (2006). *Reading research at work: Foundations of effective practice.* New York: Guilford Press.

Stanovich, K. E., & Stanovich, P. J. (2006). Fostering the scientific study of reading instruction by example. In K. A. D. Stahl & M. C. McKenna (Eds.), *Reading research at work: Foundations of effective practice* (pp. 36–44). New

York: Guilford Press.

Stanovich, P. J., & Stanovich, K. E. (2003). *Using research and reason in education: How teachers can use scientifically based research to make curricular and instructional decisions*. Portsmouth, NH: National Institute for Literacy.

Task Force of the Professional Standards and Ethics Committee of the International Reading Association. (2004). *Standards for reading professionals— Revised 2003*. Retrieved February 11, 2006, from http://www.reading.org/resources/issues/reports/professional_standards.html.

ငၽ 13

ETHICS IN EDUCATIONAL RESEARCH AND RESEARCH EDUCATION
Putting Students First

Kelly B. Cartwright

The secret of education lies in respecting the pupil.

—*Ralph Waldo Emerson*

Chapter Overview

- Our different perspectives as teachers and researchers affect the ethical decisions we make.
- Respect for students is central to the ethical guidelines of a variety of professional organizations.
- Respect for students can guide ethical decisions in educational research and practice.

Inspirational Reflection

I am an associate professor of psychology at a small, liberal arts university in Virginia. I regularly conduct research in elementary schools, and I teach research, both inside and outside of the university classroom. The "outside classroom" research education is accomplished by involving university students as research assistants in my own research program. This is the vantage point from which I write this chapter: that of educational researcher and research educator. This perspective may be beneficial, as I tend to view the research process not only from the perspective of a researcher but also from the perspective of learners who are trying to understand the research process. This perspective may also be limiting, however, because I am less aware of the unique challenges of elementary and secondary classroom teacher researchers. I try to overcome this limitation by working directly with teachers as they implement my research in their classrooms and listening carefully to teacher perspectives as we work together in the research process.

As is typical of liberal arts universities across the country, our campus community values liberal learning, which "emphasizes breadth and balance in the academic experience ... encourages students to empower themselves intellectually and practically, [and encourages students] to understand and be responsible citizens of the world in which they live" (Christopher Newport University, 2005). According to Albert Einstein, "the value of an education in a liberal arts college is not the learning of many facts, but the training of the mind to think something that cannot be learned from textbooks" (Frank, 2002, p. 105). Consistent with this educational philosophy, our campus community strives to uphold five core values of liberal learning. The first and most often cited of these is "students first." This phrase means different things to different people, depending upon who is reading it (as with most texts!). Some university students may like to think that "students first" means that faculty or staff should affirm all of their requests or demands. Most students, faculty, and staff, however, have a different interpretation. For these individuals, "students first" means that students' education and learning come first. The advancement of knowledge and student growth come first. My purpose in writing this chapter is to illustrate the parallels in educational research and research education by expanding on this core value of liberal learning. The quote from Ralph Waldo Emerson (as cited in Gilman, 2003, p. 475) with which I introduced this chapter captures the spirit of this value, which is fundamental to ethics in educational research: we respect students as students, valuing their learning and growth, whether they are students in our classes or participants in our research.

As an associate professor of psychology, I teach courses in child development, cognitive development (with an accompanying laboratory), and research methods in our undergraduate psychology curriculum. Many of the students in these courses are pursuing careers in teaching, and many seek admission to our interdisciplinary Master of Arts in Teaching program, for which I teach graduate courses in reading acquisition and development. I came to my current position by way of training as an experimental (or research) psychologist, whose work focused on children's cognitive, language, and literacy development. My graduate training, and the years after graduate school, involved much research with children in university laboratories, preschools, and elementary schools as well as research with college students in university settings. I have investigated such topics as preschool children's vocabulary development, the influence of father involvement on elementary school children's reading skills and attitudes, and the cognitive processes involved in skilled reading. My most recent work has focused on the role of cognitive flexibility—the ability to consider simultaneously multiple features of a task—in reading skill, and I have found that training in reading-specific cognitive flexibility produces improvements in elementary children's reading comprehension (Cartwright, 2002, 2006).

In addition to my teaching and research, I have also had the opportunity to serve on, and chair, the institutional review board at my university: the body that reviews research proposals to ensure the protection of participants in research. Thus, my views of ethics in research have been influenced by guidelines from several organizations: the American Psychological Association (2002), the Society for Research in Child Development (1991), and the U.S. Department of Health and Human Services, Office of Human Research Protections (2005). You can find links to the ethical guidelines for these groups in the supplementary resources section at the end of this chapter. These organizations' ethical guidelines are quite similar to those of the American Educational Research Association (see Chapter 1). Respect for participants is central to each.

What does this mean for me as an ethical educator? Students and their education come first in research and teaching. The ultimate goal of my research endeavors is to advance knowledge in the service of better education for all students. This means that I respect the students who are participants in my research, which sometimes requires that I put their needs before the goals of the research or convenience of the researcher. And, in the service of putting students' education first, I involve university students in authentic research experiences, providing them opportunities to participate in all phases of the research process—from making hypotheses and testing participants to presenting and publishing findings—to provide optimal learning experiences for these students as future researchers and educators. This sometimes means that I may spend a certain amount of time educating university students in various aspects of the research process when I could opt for the quicker and more convenient alternative of completing research tasks myself. "Tell me and I forget. Show me and I remember. Involve me and I understand." This Chinese proverb powerfully illustrates the potential of authentic experiences for optimal understanding of the research process.

Challenges and Strategies Relating to Ethical Decision Making

In this section I present several vignettes that illustrate challenges I have experienced in educational research or research education. In each of these situations you will see that the students' needs or desires conflicted with the immediate goals of the research. After describing each vignette, I explain how I handled each of these situations by finding solutions compatible with the value of respecting students, putting students and their educational needs first. In these vignettes, students' names and details of their cases have been changed to protect their identities.

Fatigued First Grader

The challenge. Several years ago I was conducting a study of first- and second-grade children's reading skills and attitudes. Each child participant in the study was tested individually and completed a series of tasks that took almost an hour to finish. To inspire children to complete the tasks, we offered them stickers and pencils for their participation (stickers and pencils seem to be especially motivating for first and second graders!), but even these incentives did not work all of the time. One little first grader, "Thomas," was working with me on these tasks in his school cafeteria. Toward the end of the session, Thomas had completed all of the research tasks with the exception of the cognitive flexibility tasks, which would take about ten minutes to complete. At this point Thomas decided, "I'm tired. I think I'm ready to go back to class." The cognitive flexibility data were particularly interesting for me as a researcher, as they had direct bearing on my main line of research. Thus, this situation created a conflict between my need for data as a researcher and Thomas's fatigue and desire to return to class.

The solution. This challenge is very typical of research with young children (or, perhaps, even typical in teaching young children). Even with incentives, these little participants find it difficult to sit through a long research session. Ethically, even when we have parent or teacher permission for participation, children have the right to withdraw from our studies without negative consequences. When Thomas requested that he return to class, I told him that we were "almost done" and asked whether he was sure he wanted to stop. He said, "yes," and we walked back to his class. Of course, I gave him his sticker and pencil for participating. In this case, to respect the child's needs, I had to allow his fatigue and desire to discontinue participation to supersede my need for interesting data.

Inequitable Improvements

The challenge. Recently, I worked with some reading teacher colleagues on an intervention study with struggling readers at a local elementary school. We implemented a teacher-administered, small-group version of the reading-specific flexibility intervention I had developed for individual administration

(Cartwright, 2002, 2006). Because the individual intervention was effective in improving reading comprehension, we had the reasonable expectation that the small-group intervention would produce similar improvements. This presented a challenge. To do sound research we needed an intervention group (children who received the small-group reading-specific flexibility intervention) and a control group (children who did not receive the intervention, with whose performance we could compare the performance of the intervention children). But, because the intervention had the potential to improve children's performance, we were faced with the inequitable outcome of offering improvements to some children, while offering no improvements for others.

The solution. In this case students' educational needs were conflicting with the need to design sound research. To respect our research participants, we felt we should offer equivalent benefits to all children involved in the study. This is exactly the solution we chose. We pre-tested intervention and control children on reading skill, implemented the intervention with the intervention group over a five-week period while the control group received regular small-group reading lessons. Then, we post-tested children on reading skills after the intervention was complete. As we expected, the children who had received the intervention scored significantly higher on school- and researcher-administered measures of reading comprehension (Cartwright et al., 2006). To ensure that all children in the study received the same benefits, we provided the reading-specific flexibility intervention to the children in the control group once post-testing was complete. In this way we preserved the integrity of the research process while respecting the children's need for, and right to, equitable educational improvements.

Uncertain Undergraduates

The challenge. As a professor who involves university students as assistants in research, I am faced with learning how to include a variety of individuals in the research process in meaningful ways. University students' individual strengths vary, and so do their levels of comfort with research tasks. Occasionally, even after I provide extensive training to research assistants on experimental tasks, such as reading and cognitive assessments, I find that the research assistants just aren't adequately prepared to administer the tasks to participants. One assistant, for example, had great difficulty learning to pronounce words in a nonword reading task. Another assistant felt that he was not comfortable enough with the task protocols to work with actual participants. Nevertheless, these students were quite interested in learning about the research process and wanted to be involved in my research team.

The solution. In cases such as these, my need for appropriately prepared research assistants conflicted with the university students' strengths and comfort levels with research tasks. This situation is much like that experienced by a classroom teacher who finds that her or his students come with different levels of skill and preparation for class assignments. One way to meet the needs of different students while accomplishing educational goals is to implement differentiated instruction (Tomlinson, 2000). This is exactly the solution I chose. Rather than assign student research assistants to tasks for which they were inadequately prepared or with which they were uncomfortable, I sought to place these students in tasks more suited to their individual needs. Data collection—that is, testing research participants—is just one of the many tasks necessary for the smooth operation of a research program. Other tasks essential to this process include literature review, stimulus construction, test scoring, and data entry. By assigning these university students to other tasks for which they were more prepared or with which they were more comfortable, I was able to meet their educational needs, respect their preferences, and preserve the integrity of the research process.

Synthesis of Ethical Lessons Learned

Before I was asked to write this chapter, I had not considered the similarities in educational research and research education. In doing so I have found that two important aspects of my professional life, teaching and conducting research, have much in common. The purpose of educational research is to advance knowledge of student learning to benefit as many students as possible. That is, students' learning comes first. In the case of research education, student learning is also a primary goal. In both situations, whether interacting with research participants or university students, respect for students is essential. As the vignettes I presented in this chapter demonstrate, the goals of research and the needs of students may sometimes conflict. If we keep respect for students foremost in practice, however, we can optimize student learning while preserving the integrity of the research process. As Emerson noted, "The secret of education lies in respecting the pupil." I would expand this to suggest that the secret of educational research and research education lies in putting students first.

Questions for Consideration

Consider how your perspective as a teacher or researcher affects your students.

Do your students view your research as something they would value?

Reflect on the ways you strive to put your students' learning first in your educational practice.

Have you encountered situations in which your students had different levels of comfort or preparedness for learning tasks? How did you handle these differences?

Have you encountered situations when your goals as a teacher or researcher conflicted with your students' needs? How did you handle these situations?

Supplementary Resources

Ethical Guidelines from Other Organizations: American Psychological Association. (2002). *Ethical principles of psychologists and code of conduct.* Retrieved January 30, 2007, from http://www.apa.org/ethics; Society for Research in Child Development. (1991). *Ethical standards for research with children.* Retrieved January 30, 2007, from http://srcd.org/ethicalstandards.html; U. S. Department of Health and Human Services. (2005). *Protection of human subjects* (Code of Federal Regulations, Title 45, Part 46). Retrieved January 30, 2007, from http://www.hhs.gov/ohrp/humansubjects/guidance/45cfr46.htm.

Resources on Differentiated Instruction: The Reading Rockets Web site has a number of good resources on differentiated instruction: instruction that is tailored to meet individual students' needs. Search for "Differentiated Instruction" at http://readingrockets.org.

Tomlinson, C. A. (2000). What is differentiated instruction? Retrieved February 4, 2007, from http://www.readingrockets.org/article/263. This article by Dr. Carol Ann Tomlinson may be especially helpful.

References

Cartwright, K. B. (2002). Cognitive development and reading: The relation of reading-specific multiple classification skill to reading comprehension in elementary school children. *Journal of Educational Psychology, 94,* 56–63.

————. (2006). Fostering flexibility and comprehension in elementary students. *The Reading Teacher, 59,* 628–634.

Cartwright, K. B., Schmidt, K., Clause, J., Price, G., & Thomas, S. (2006). Small group reading-specific flexibility intervention for struggling readers

(In process).

Christopher Newport University. (2005). *Liberal learning core curriculum*. Retrieved February 2, 2007, from http://liberallearning.cnu.edu.

Frank, P. (2002). *Einstein, his life and times*. Cambridge, MA: Da Capo Press.

Gilman, W. H. (Ed.). (2003). *Selected writings of Ralph Waldo Emerson*. New York, NY: Penguin Group.

Tomlinson, C. A. (2000). What is differentiated instruction? Retrieved February 4, 2007, from http://www.readingrockets.org/article/263.

๙ *14*

The Ethical Dilemmas of Teacher Research as a Research Agenda

Neal Shambaugh

And be one traveler, long I stood.

—*Robert Frost*

Chapter Overview

- This chapter reminds readers about the ethical dilemmas inherent in using teacher research in one's research agendas, particularly at research universities.

Inspirational Reflection

"The Road Not Taken" by Robert Frost (1920) is a commonly quoted poem regarding one's choices in life, especially the lines "Two roads diverged in a wood, and I— / I took the one less traveled by, / And that has made all the difference." The poem also urges one to commit to a path. If one reads the whole poem the words "And be one traveler, long I stood" depict a new faculty member who must decide on a scholarly path, shaded on one side by the question of "What counts as research?" and illuminated on the other side by one's scholarly agenda. One possible way along this path is teacher research. For some faculty members, the study of teaching is a moral endeavor, as one's teaching impacts others. Pragmatic issues of "what counts as research" influence the choices of what to study and what research road to take; thus, the line "And be one traveler, long I stood" seems to characterize this ethical dilemma.

The first time I stood at this crossroads was in 1971 after completing student teaching in a fifth-grade open classroom, an experience that exhausted me but was personally and professionally fulfilling by the end of the day. However, by the end of the semester, I opted out of teaching. I chose instead to start a program in engineering, but then dropped out and owned two businesses. Subsequently, I worked for fifteen years in a land-grant university as a video producer, during which time I completed a business degree and entered graduate school. As a student again I found myself taking notes on how the instructors were teaching, as well as what content was being taught. Twenty-five years after student teaching I found myself traveling full circle back into teaching again, but this time in a college classroom.

An exemplary college teacher provided me with opportunities to teach alongside her and jointly conduct teacher research that was regularly disseminated at research conferences. As a faculty member myself, I have come to realize how time-consuming and potentially risky her decision was. Each course delivery involved weekly meetings on what the teaching should involve, how the learning tasks should be structured, how students were coping with the tasks and learning the content, and what adjustments we needed to make. Several of my peers were surprised that my dissertation would not be about the textbook we coauthored. I chose, rather, to document the five-year study of teaching a course and how a reflexive teaching model developed (Shambaugh & Magliaro, 2001). The model depicted students and instructors as joint learners with similar characteristics but with different roles and discussed how, through different forms of participation structures, we learned alongside students. Our reflexive stance, however, necessitated that we encounter ethical dilemmas.

Challenges Related to Ethical Decision Making

Challenge 1: Becoming explicit about one's foundations for teaching and learning.

One of the first teaching strategies that I learned from coteaching was establishing in each course a *starting point*, the logic being that before progress can be achieved, one needs to know where one has been and where one is at. Students identify one to three words that describe themselves as teachers, their views of students, and their views of themselves as learners. Educators may unconsciously operate from a deficit model, which in turn may be based on unclear learning outcomes, fuzzy assessment, and unorganized tasks and schedules. Related "starting point" activities have included an educational philosophy, a designer's mission statement, and personalized planning/designing models.

These "starting point" activities place students' teaching and learning beliefs "on the table" and show how their teaching decisions are based on these beliefs, some of which are tacitly held and have gone unexamined. Students can then see how their teaching and learning beliefs match up with learning principles, which are based on learning theories. In this way, their theoretical foundation for teaching is developed *from* their beliefs, rather than the other way around. Their theoretical foundation typically draws on several learning theories.

I also explain my theoretical foundation for teaching and learning, the rationale for tasks and how they are structured, and how learning will be assessed. By doing so, I share my teaching decisions, ask for students' feedback, and prompt them to "take notes" mentally on my teaching. On the syllabus, course outcomes are paired with student performance requirements; thus, the alignment of learning with assessment is clearly communicated. An assessment plan provides details. Providing my theoretical foundation and helping students to develop their own sets the stage for individual or joint teacher research.

Challenge 2: Modeling good teaching and modeling inquiry into one's teaching.

Modeling good teaching involves many personal traits, dispositions, and sensibilities, as well as skills. The definition of good teaching is sometimes confused with what makes an effective teacher. In my experience many teachers see these notions as the same. I view teaching as requiring personal dispositions and learned skills. Teacher research also involves a desire to improve as an educator and the skills needed to choose, frame, and conduct a study. Modeling of teaching and inquiry can continue at a higher level of student–instructor participation, providing a more authentic experience of what it means to be a college teacher.

As with one's theoretical foundation, teacher research can be shared in class. Teacher research can be conducted with other students, now that they have experienced the course as students. Joint research may be risky with graduate students, as it requires mutual investment of additional time and trust, with the possibility of miscommunication, disappointment, and dead-ends along the way. As teaching involves daily risk taking, so does collaborating with new colleagues. These risks must be taken and cannot be sidestepped.

One of the ethical dilemmas with studying teaching in higher education is sometimes experiencing resistance from one's peers. I find it an irony in a college of education that faculty members are not conducting self-studies of their own teaching. The notion of studying one's teaching using research methodologies comes as a surprise to some faculty members. I conduct short seminars with faculty members on ways to study one's own teaching. I usually provide a broad overview of ways to do this, such as Bullough and Gitlin's (1995) coverage, ranging from teaching metaphors to curriculum analysis to action research. I then provide an overview of developmental research, which involves a three-stage cycle of documentation and analysis. In the first stage teaching decisions are recorded. A second stage records teaching implementation and adjustments. The third stage evaluates student learning and student perceptions of their learning and my teaching. Evaluation results then feed back into future course decisions (Richey, Klein, & Nelson, 2003). Such an approach ensures that one documents the full range of developmental decisions and provides a rich descriptive history from which more specialized research can be conducted.

Challenge 3: Being a responsive teacher and advisor.

From my earliest days of student teaching in a fifth-grade classroom, I learned that paying attention to students required more time than I had thought but that the efforts usually paid off. In one case, I worked one on one with a boy who did not engage with the other students. One day after school I had him remove everything from inside his extremely messy desk. I asked him to explain the value of each item before returning it to his desk. Most of the materials were thrown away. The stories he told me about the materials helped me to get to know this boy. The messy desk represented where this student was and where I needed to be. What I learned then and what I continue to learn to this day is the value of learning as much about one's students as possible and what is in their world.

To understand my students' world, I remind them to remind me about what is going on in their lives and "what is on their plate." This information, which is gathered continuously, helps to adjust activity and task schedules. To accommodate shifts in a course, a certain amount of "slack" needs to be designed into the schedule, initially taking into account the semester calendar, major holidays, and student benchmark dates across other courses. Responsive teaching also requires careful listening and frequent checking for student understanding. Overall, the payoff is better thinking and better work from students. Responsive teaching requires feedback that is timely and connected with due dates. Feedback must address student accomplishments and areas for improvement and provide meaningful comments beyond writing "Good Work." Feedback must be consistent. Suggestions that approve student work at one point should not contradict the student at a later point.

Ethical Teaching Strategies

One can summarize additional teaching strategies as they apply to ethical teaching and teacher research by examining events across one's teaching trajectory. In my initial reflection, I had to make a decision about what teaching was needed for a fifth-grade boy who had some self-esteem issues. For this student to move forward, I had to help him find his own "starting point." This was my first experience in realizing that "content" might involve more than content areas. Teaching, consequently, must address this content. And, most important, to learn about this full range of content, one needs to learn about students. This particular case provided me with my own starting point, where I was to resume many years later.

When afforded the opportunity to teach alongside my doctoral advisor, I was pretty terrified. Who was I to teach other teachers? She provided me with a timely book by Duckworth titled *The Having of Wonderful Ideas*. Duckworth (1987) wrote about a view of teaching that gave me the courage to step back into the classroom:

> By teacher, I mean someone who engages learners, who seeks to involve each person wholly . . . and having engaged the learners, a teacher finds his questions to be the same as those that a researcher might into the nature of human understanding and wants to ask: What do you think and why? While the student learns, the teacher learns too. (p. 134)

As a former radio announcer with a keen sense of audience, I realized that "I can do this. I can help students engage in their own learning!" Little did I know that the teacher-research stance would develop into a reflexive approach to teaching where I made explicit decisions about learning alongside students. In working with experienced teachers, a useful strategy is the critical incident technique in which one recounts an experience where one's sense of being a teacher is tested. This occurred for me during graduate student teaching when one of my student peers refused to be assessed by me. A typical strategy for us was to use personal conferences to discuss student progress and concerns. During this conference, this student refused to talk. Not a word was uttered for more than thirty minutes. We managed to keep the conversation focused on learning and I remember saying, "If there is no dialogue, we cannot help you." In this class we had shared our theoretical foundations, one of which was our view of teaching as "assisting performance," an idea from Tharp and Gallimore (1988). After two days of mental paralysis, I realized that nineteen other students in the course needed my assistance.

As I moved from graduate student to faculty member, I took on master's and doctoral advisees, and looked forward to sharing with them the richness of my experience. I came to learn that not all advisees were like me and that my experience could not be theirs. I discovered that there was no formula that could be applied to all advisees and that the advising process was fraught with internal issues such as when to intervene, how they think and work, how much time should be invested in this person, and when to suggest that maybe another faculty member is needed. I find advising to be my toughest teaching challenge. With a heavy doctoral advising load, it feels like the same people are taking the same "course" for three to five years and nobody hands anything in. I want to pay attention, but I'm bedeviled with the question of "who motivates whom?" At the graduate level, I realized that not everyone can do this work and that one has to like the work and be willing to pay the price to complete a program. This issue remains for me an unresolved ethical dilemma.

I promote teacher research on three fronts. The first is reminding tenure-track faculty members that disseminating one's teaching, particularly in a college or school of education, can "count" toward tenure. My message is aimed not at promoting a particular research methodology but at showing that teacher research can be a productive activity if a new faculty member writes out a research agenda and a publication plan and then gets organized and "works" his or her plan. The second front is working in a five-year teacher education program where action research is required for a master's degree. Modeling my own teacher research makes it easy for me to ask new teachers to conduct theirs. Advising them remains a challenge in terms of identifying a study, unpacking its assumptions, and carrying it out and writing about it (Shambaugh & Webb-Dempsey, in press). However, one of the many messages that surrounds new teachers is that teacher research is outside of teaching and just "one more thing to do." Teaching and advising in this area requires that one truly believes in teacher research and has conducted it in order to understand the challenges of implementing systematic inquiry in a classroom. A third front for teacher research involves my university-wide efforts to improve teaching. This effort requires a slow "sell" over time to gain the trust of faculty members and department heads from other units. "An hour here, an hour there" over many years is necessary.

Synthesis of Ethical Lessons Learned

The ethical lessons that I have learned from the blending of teaching and teacher research can be summarized in terms of trust and reflexivity, and for both there exist risks and rewards.

Early in my graduate student years, I realized that somewhere along the line we have to trust our colleagues and students, but that there would be risks in doing so. Building trust we know takes time and sincerity, but the rewards of doing so are opportunities to get better at teaching. Building trust with students means paying attention, and mutual trust is earned with engagement, fairness, and performance. However, not all students will buy into this set of accommodations. The starting point activities mentioned earlier are attempts at helping students to define themselves, what Grudin (1990) describes as a "formidable challenge" and potentially risky for an instructor to question educators' views of their role.

Reflexivity, I learned from my first days as a student teacher in fifth grade, required a genuine disposition to learn alongside a student. Desire, however, is not enough. To understand the term, one has to experience reflexivity and understand that these experiences will take many years. A reflexive teaching model required five years of teacher research, but the sustained focus provided me with productive work habits and a rich descriptive base to examine teaching decisions. Different forms of participation structures for students (Wenger, 1998) were examined, including texts, in-class activities, personal conferences, projects, Web boards, Web sites, and collaborative Web pages. A view of teaching as assisting student performance widened the teaching options from just instructing to modeling, to cognitive structuring, and to reflecting (Tharp & Gallimore, 1988).

The value of locking risk taking and reflexivity arm in arm is to remind me that I am on a road, albeit one that is risky and perilous, and both shaded and illuminated with uncertainty and possibility. In writing this essay, I realized that I was experiencing the content of what it means to be a faculty member and thus living within my own research question where teaching and teacher research inform each other. I know that not all students will take advantage of trust in the right ways. Not all peers will value inquiry into teaching. Not all reflexivity of teaching and teacher research will yield results that are clear or predictable. This particular road taken, that of teaching and the study of one's teaching, remains a risky decision, but deciding to move forward in some direction and moving beyond where "long I stood" remains the hardest and most important decision.

Questions for Consideration

Who am I as a teacher? Record one to three words that describe you as a teacher, your views of students, and your views of yourself as a learner. List and write about the critical incidents that have shaped your development as a teacher.

How do I want to be successful? Write out your research agenda, research sites, and publication schedule.

How do I want to study my teaching? Make a list of courses and other opportunities to study your teaching, either alone or with others. Compare this list with your research agenda and see how they might overlap.

How do I work? Make a list of organization strategies you will use to work your research/teaching agenda.

Supplementary Resources

Teaching: Shulman, L. S. (2004). *Teaching as community property: Essays on higher education.* San Francisco: Jossey-Bass; Shulman, L. S. (2004). *The wisdom of practice: Essays on teaching, learning, and learning to teach.* San Francisco: Jossey-Bass. These companion sets of essays provide me with encouraging grounding in the scope and significance of teaching. Shulman was a gift from my doctoral advisor.

Mentoring: Sinetar, M. (1998). *The mentor's spirit: Life lessons on leadership and the art of encouragement.* New York: St. Martin's Griffin. A book to be read between semesters or when the going gets tough during semesters.

Teacher Research: Bullough, R. V., Jr., & Gitlin, A. (1995). *Becoming a student of teaching: Methodologies for exploring self and school context.* New York: Garland. A useful text for teachers who want to study their teaching individually or collectively.

References

Bullough, Jr., R. V., & Gitlin, A. (1995). *Becoming a student of teaching: Methodologies for exploring self and school context.* New York: Garland.

Duckworth, E. (1987). *The having of wonderful ideas and other essays on teaching and learning.* New York: Teachers College Press.

Frost, R. (1920). *Mountain interval.* New York: Henry Holt and Company.

Grudin, R. (1990). *The grace of great things: Creativity and imagination.* New York: Ticknor and Fields.

Richey, R. C., Klein, J. D., & Nelson, W. A. (2003). Developmental research. In D. H. Jonassen (Ed.), *Handbook of research for educational communications and technology* (2nd ed.) (pp. 1099–1130). Mahwah, NJ: Lawrence Erlbaum.

Shambaugh, R. N., & Magliaro, S. (2001). A reflexive model for teaching and learning instructional design. *Educational Technology Research & Development, 49*(2), 69–92.

Shambaugh, R. N., & Webb-Dempsey, J. (in press). Focusing the study: Framing a researchable question. In C. A. Lassonde & S. E. Israel (Eds.), *Handbook of teacher research*. Newark, DE: International Reading Association (2008).

Tharp, R. G., & Gallimore, R. (1988). *Rousing minds to life: Teaching, learning, and school in social context*. Cambridge, UK: Cambridge University Press.

Wenger, E. (1998). *Communities of practice: Learning, meaning, and identity*. New York: Cambridge University Press.

৫ *15*

STUDENT TEACHERS, TEACHER RESEARCH, AND ETHICS

Linda Pratt and Kenneth J. Weiss

> Ethics is in origin the art of recommending to others the sacrifices required for cooperation with oneself.
>
> *—Bertrand Russell*

> Education is the art of making [people] ethical.
>
> *—Georg Hagel*

> Action indeed is the sole medium of expression for ethics.
>
> *—Jane Adams*

Chapter Overview

- What ethical challenges do teacher education students, and in particular student teachers, face?
- What ethical dilemmas and decisions do we as teachers commonly experience because of what we do?
- How can we mentor teacher education students, in particular student teachers, to help them develop an ethical sense and learn how to rely on it when deciding what they should or should not do as teachers and learners?

Inspirational Reflection

For several years we have witnessed teacher education students entering college who either had committed plagiarism themselves or were aware of high school peers who did (Strom & Strom, 2007). In the rite of passage from high school to college, these same students quickly realize that their high school experiences with plagiarism can and do transfer to academic life on a college campus (Hutton, 2006). As an example, before teacher education students begin student teaching, we often ask them to be reflective about their on-campus and in-school field experiences. These range from writing reflections regarding on-campus peer simulations to writing apprentice case studies about pupils they are mentoring in literacy in school.

For the most part, our students' work serves as a valid indicator of their own understanding of theory and practice and is authentic and reflective in nature. Furthermore, most of the students' behaviors and work display high degrees of ethical behavior, on campus and in school. However, occasionally, we come across case studies based on scenarios that are recycled versions of someone else's prior work, lesson plans that are clearly copied from the Internet without citations, reflections that were previously submitted by peers, and papers certain students could not have written on the basis of previous writing samples.

Although our previously mentioned experiences with ethical issues in our teachings are neither new nor unique, the ethical decisions that student teachers face are different and encompass a broad range of concerns, including their future as ethical teacher researchers. One such concern is the difficult responsibility of monitoring and guiding their own pupils' ethical behaviors, as well as testing and improving their own ethical sense. Student teachers who may have cheated on an exam or plagiarized in high school or even in college now have to deal with these ethical transgressions from the perspective of a teacher. What was once acceptable, if not expected, behavior now becomes unacceptable. How do student teachers resolve the hypocrisy of requiring and cultivating ethical reasoning and action in their own pupils and in themselves as prospective professionals in light of their past or even current ethical transgressions as students?

Another issue is that with the intense teaching demands placed on student teachers, coupled with the overwhelming need to succeed in student teaching, we have observed student teachers who previously relied on unethical behaviors to succeed face additional serious issues and consequences. If their ethical transgressions are uncovered, they risk failing student teaching and not being able to enter the profession. Conversely, if they diligently uphold generally accepted ethical standards, they feel disadvantaged and, therefore, may fail student teaching by being ethical.

If we accept that ethics guide our teaching and our students' learning, then we must closely examine how ethics is defined and practiced. In the introduction to this book, Israel uses *Merriam-Webster's Collegiate Dictionary*, 11th edition, to define ethics as the discipline dealing with what is good and bad and with moral duty and obligation.

Likewise, the practice of ethics requires that all educators be exposed to, and learn how to commit to, codes of ethics throughout their academic and teaching careers. Many student teachers initially learn about dress codes that are required in the schools where they student teach. They do not seem to realize, however, that a particular school district's ethical code is only a local manifestation of a more general set of ethical principles and professional standards to which all teachers are expected to adhere. Hence, student teachers need to understand that codes of ethics exist at local, state (e.g., New York State Education Department of Higher Learning), and national (e.g., National Education Association) levels. Moreover, ethical behavior is a prominent concern and goal of any academic discipline (e.g., the International Reading Association). By informing students early on about ethical codes of conduct, by modeling ethical decision making and actions, and by expecting students to practice ethical standards rigorously, we can better explain to our students why ethics is fundamental to teaching and learning and why it is imperative to follow faithfully what they decide is the ethical thing to do—not to avoid rebuke or gain reward but simply to do what is right for any teacher to do in a given situation.

If we believe that all teachers should embrace teacher research throughout their professional lives, then all student teachers should learn not only how to define and practice ethical decision making before and during student teaching but also how to acquire a foundation upon which to become a principled teacher researcher. After all, do we not agree that truly useful and credible teacher research must emanate from individuals who hold to high professional and ethical standards in all aspects of research?

Challenges Related to Ethical Decision Making

There are many challenges to guiding preservice teachers, and in particular student teachers, to adopt and practice ethical decision making and behaviors. As experienced teachers, we begin teaching our students about ethics by modeling how to think and act ethically, in contrast to their unethical decisions and behaviors. First, students' prior and current experiences with unethical behaviors too often result in few, if any, penalties of meaningful consequence. The main reason our students act unethically is because they believe that their peers generally cheat in some way and, therefore, rationalize that academic dishonesty is a justifiable and "smart" means (if undetected) to a desired end, namely to get a good grade. Thus, it is hard to convince students to act ethically when ethical transgressions seem justifiable or expedient, particularly when the perceived personal benefits of unethical actions are high relative to the costs. This is especially true when a low grade-point average can lead not only to loss of academic scholarships and privileges but also to being rejected for student teaching.

Another challenge that we have experienced is how we should decide what to do when confronted with an ethical dilemma. For example, what factors and effects should we weigh when deciding what to do when students falsify a case study and claim it is their work alone? First, we may decide whether it is worth taking the time from our busy schedules to collect evidence of plagiarism and fabricated research findings. Then, how much more time and effort should we expend when the initial evidence is inconclusive? Next, we may consider the effect on other students in the class if we decide whether to penalize a student for an ethical transgression. Similarly, what does a teacher decide to do when the ethical offense occurs midway through the course? Will the guilty student sway peers to view us as acting unfairly or being excessively "uptight" about ethics? Will one or more members of the class react resentfully, challenge our authority to demand ethical accountability, and thereby undermine the course? What will be the effect of enforcing strict ethical standards on students' evaluations of us and our course? Moreover, how will the exercise of our ethical principles, or lack thereof, in the classroom affect our prospects for tenure or promotion? Finally, when we judge whether a student acted unethically, we are apt to weigh what happens to such a student. For example, we might excuse ethical misconduct when the penalties are severe and impose consequences only when they are light. These consequences can include failing an assignment, failing the course, losing a scholarship, or dismissal from the institution. Likewise, the effect of not enforcing ethical standards in the classroom should be considered as well. For example, what might be the outcome of ignoring suspected ethical transgressions? If students continue to behave unethically without being held accountable, their peers may perceive the lack of real penalties as an implicit license to act unethically when it seems in their interest to do so. At least equally troubling are the unethical students graduating and becoming teachers.

One actual situation that tested strict observance of high ethical standards was the student teacher who, at the end of student teaching, submitted two plagiarized lesson plan reflections, which apparently he had never done before. Furthermore, the student was the sole supporter of his two children, had an extremely ill spouse, had been offered a teaching job, and had been a model student and inspiration to others in the class. Should we fail students in similar situations and, thereby, effectively bar them from teaching careers? Are there other, less severe options? How important is it to be consistent in our decision making as we recall past students who for one ethical transgression or another failed to complete the education major or even to graduate? How will cooperating teachers and colleagues view our responses to unethical behavior in our students?

In addition to the impact that our ethical decision making has on our students and on ourselves, the ethical or unethical actions of our colleagues should require our attention. We have worked with a few colleagues who do not make ethically sound decisions. Such individuals, for example, ignore students' unethical behaviors for a variety of reasons. They may believe that it is futile to demand they follow ethical norms inside as well as outside class or that it is not worth investing time and energy to enforce such demands, or they may fear that being ethically "uptight" might cost them popularity among their students. Regardless of the reasons, a few of our colleagues have diluted our efforts to model ethical decision making and acting accordingly, and consequently tend to perpetuate an ethical blindness or insensitivity in developing new teachers.

The effect that these challenges have had on our professional development and ethical sense are far-reaching. As we make hard ethical decisions as teacher researchers, we reflect upon the direct and indirect ramifications of those decisions on our integrity as teachers, on our students' education, on our colleagues' attitudes, and on how others perceive our profession. Moreover, we have learned that thoughtful analysis of our decision-making process in ethically problematic situations has enabled us to make better decisions in the future. Thus, each time we apply our ethical sense to decide what we should or should not do, we become better teacher researchers and add an ethical dimension to our philosophical views of what it means to teach, to learn, and to be an educated person.

Ethical Teaching Strategies

In working with student teachers and observing their ethical practices, it is readily apparent that we, as teacher educators and researchers, need to integrate ethics into their preparation from the outset of their program. It is paramount that we help students understand what ethics is and why it is important, what the teaching profession demands of teachers ethically speaking, and how ethics affects them as student teachers and as future teacher researchers.

One strategy that we have used is to question our students about the reasons behind their ethical or unethical behaviors. We also try to model ethical behavior in our classrooms and to explain why and when it is important to follow ethical guidelines as teachers as well as students. We often relate stories of our own research and writing to illustrate and explain why ethics and honesty in teaching and in teacher research are vital to education.

Another of our practices is to engage our students in ethical discussions concerning their own work and, in turn, their expectations for the pupils they will teach in their own classrooms. For instance, if it were acceptable in their eyes as students to copy all or part of an assignment from an unidentified source, how then would they react to their students doing the same thing? Do we practice what we preach, or do we just pay lip service to an ethical code when it is convenient or in our narrow self-interest to do so?

We also find that providing students with interactive case study opportunities is a productive way to deal with the importance of learning and applying ethical decision making. In addition, role-playing techniques seem to help students better understand ways to identify critical ethical issues and how to resolve them successfully.

What also appears to be successful is embedding in the content of our classes various aspects of how one becomes and remains an ethical agent. By presenting plausible scenarios involving ethical decision making in field placement and student teaching situations, we encourage our students to explore and discuss potential actions and outcomes to understand better the issues and how they might be settled and ethically justified.

Getting others involved in ethics instruction is another useful approach. For example, we use teacher education clubs, education honor societies, and student teachers to inform their peers, especially first-year students, about ethics in the context of roundtable discussions. Also, asking practicing teachers and administrators to share relevant experiences with student teachers who have had to face ethical dilemmas further appears to exert a strong influence on teacher education students. Regardless of the method we use to promote and teach ethics, we believe that the time and effort we invest to do so contributes to our teacher education students becoming more ethical student teachers, teachers, and ultimately teacher researchers.

Synthesis of Ethical Lessons Learned

Instruction in ethics should begin in introductory education courses and continue throughout student teaching. Such instruction should meld ethical theory with practice so that students learn not only what ethical reasoning entails but also how to apply it.

Making choices on the basis of ethical considerations and acting accordingly can be difficult for anyone. Part of ethical decision making requires consideration of conflicting factors, such as short- versus long-term effects, personal versus social impacts, and tangible versus intangible consequences. The personal consequences of being ethical (or unethical) are most immediate and apparent; the impact on others, commonly less obvious and, therefore, more easily overlooked. One's decisions and actions also can impinge, sometimes subtly, on groups of people, institutions, and society as a whole.

Often, unpleasant and uncertain trade-offs have to be made when using ethical guidelines to decide how to resolve ethical dilemmas. Sometimes errors in judgment and action occur when deciding what should be done, and in some cases, there will be regrets. Education students and student teachers especially need to be mentored so they can assume the responsibility of being an ethical agent and dealing with the ramifications of doing what one thinks is best. Similarly, lessons in ethics also should remind our students that sincerely, thoughtfully trying to do the right thing not only increases our chances for success but also helps us learn how to make better decisions and act ethically, whether as a student or as a teacher.

Being ethical can be contagious. When we model ethical decision making and ethical actions, others are more likely to follow suit, including students and colleagues alike. Likewise, growing ethical acumen in some students will tend to foster a similar propensity to ethical action in their peers. Therefore, ethical instruction and practice must be integral parts of the preservice teachers' curriculum. Students benefit from understanding why ethics is important to learning as well as to teaching. They also need to learn how to apply ethical principles and norms and to refine and occasionally even reassess their growing ethical sensibilities. Lessons in ethics should include realistic, "minds-on" activities in which students test ethical reasoning skills with realistic, nontrivial case studies. It is also important to convince students that any credible and useful product of teacher research depends on adherence to ethical standards. Ideally, then, becoming ethical students will lay the foundation for becoming teachers of high professional caliber and ultimately teacher researchers who truly value and practice ethical principles.

Questions for Consideration

Reflect on how asking student teachers to analyze their own and their pupils' ethical decision-making behaviors could affect their future as teacher researchers.

In what ways could these student teacher reflections strengthen your own teacher researcher practices?

Consider how your ethical decision-making practices have changed from the time you were a student teacher to now. How have these changes strengthened you as a teacher researcher?

Supplemental Resources

Reflecting on Ethical Issues: Hammack, F. (1997). Ethical issues in teacher research. *Teachers College Record, 99*(2), 247–265.

Reflecting on the Impact of Culture and Ethics: Lieberman, A. E. (1988). *Building a professional culture in schools.* New York: Teachers College Press. Sockett, H. (1993). *The moral base for teacher professionalism.* New York: Teachers College Press.

Ethics As Professional Development: Strike, K. A. (1990). Teaching ethics to teachers: What the curriculum should be. *Teaching and Teacher Education, 6*(1), 47–53.

Strike, K. A., & Soltis, J. F. (1998). *The ethics of teaching.* New York: Teachers College Press.

Zeni, J. (1998). A guide to ethical issues and action research. *Education Action Research,* 6(1), 9–19.

References

Hutton, P. A. (2006). Understanding student cheating and what educators can do about it. *College Teaching, 54*(1), 171–177.
Strom P. S., & Strom, R. D. (2007). Cheating in middle and high school. *The Educational Forum, 71,* 104–116.

Acknowledgments

To my husband, Michael, thank you for your unwavering and unending support and encouragement. (LP)

I want to thank my wife, Bobbie, for her patience, understanding, and moral support. (KJW)

CR 16

Conclusion
Themes in Ethical Behavior in Educational Practice

Cynthia Shanahan

The educator, believing in the worth and dignity of each human being, recognizes the supreme importance of the pursuit of truth, devotion to excellence, and the nurture of the democratic principles.

—*NEA Code of Ethics of the Education Profession, Preamble*

Chapter Overview

- Responsibility to teach.
- Making ethical decisions.
- Honoring student voices.
- Honoring our colleagues' voices.

Inspirational Reflection

In my early years of teaching, I made an awful mistake. I was teaching fourth grade and my students were engaged in writing. One of them—his hair sticking on end, his shirttail half in and half out of his jeans, his shoes untied, and his face screwed up with effort—was really, really trying to make his paper readable. I walked over to him and said, "Wow! That really looks great …" He beamed. But then I finished the sentence jokingly, "… for you." He broke out in tears. I felt horrible. And it took me a long time to regain his trust. What did that I do that had to do with ethics? I wasn't careful enough to preserve his feelings. I didn't honor his starting point.

While reading these chapters in preparation for writing this final word, I was struck by the varied contexts in which ethical decision making is an issue.

Ethical (or unethical) decisions are made by individuals and groups daily, and yet the points where these decisions are made, the complexities involved in taking into account competing views, the important ways that educators demonstrate their ethics in the day-to-day practice of their profession, the sheer agony involved in making difficult decisions (where *someone* will be affected in possibly profound ways)—these points are often invisible to us, rarely laid bare for the consideration of others. Because this volume does just that, providing wonderful insights into the complexities of ethical behavior at a very personal level, it is indeed an important jumping-off point for necessary courageous conversations within the realm of educational practice.

In this final chapter, I organize my thoughts and questions around the several themes that struck me as I read across the varied contexts discussed in this book: teaching students in P–16 classrooms; teaching both teacher candidates and in-service teachers in university classrooms; providing extra support to students who need it; conducting research in teaching and learning; and engaging with a community of scholars both in and across settings. These themes are ones that particularly resonated with my experiences.

Theme One: Responsibility to Teach

Two chapters in this volume brought up the responsibilities of teachers (and teacher educators) to teach that which is called for (Goeke and Eldridge, Chapter 6, and Stahl, Chapter 12). Goeke and Eldridge discuss professors' "willful and purposeful exclusion" of knowledge teacher candidates needed that they "preferred not to teach." The obligation to teach even our least favorite topics seems foundational for ethical educators. We know, for example, that for children to read proficiently, they need to be able to pronounce words, know what they mean, read connected text fluently, and understand and think about what they are reading. To leave out any of these aspects of reading instruction would be detrimental to a child, especially one who relies on the school to teach him or her to read. That is, we could not possibly justify the teaching of phonemic awareness only or of comprehension only, even if one of those topics were a teacher's particular area of expertise and interest. Yet, in colleges of education, we often teach only those things we prefer to teach, explaining our lack of explicit instruction in non-preferred areas by calling on notions such as "academic freedom." What obligation do we have to teach preservice teachers specific strategies for teaching all aspects of literacy? As Stahl points out, explicit teaching is not often immediately rewarded. Her preservice teacher candidates, who were not previously held accountable for knowing how to do something, resisted her attempts. Yet her persistence paid off—those she taught were better prepared to take on the responsibilities for teaching the full range of reading elements to their students.

I'm sometimes mystified by my own colleagues' views about what they believe should be shared with the teacher candidates in their classes. For example, when we were discussing the professional teaching standards in our state, several of my colleagues bristled at the thought that these should be mentioned in their syllabi or in their classes. I think they believed that telling students what standards the state was expecting them to meet would somehow undermine motivation or that it would make their instruction seem too lock-step, disconnected from the big picture. Perhaps they felt that paying attention to the standards (none of which, by the way, they disagreed with) would force them into teaching "one standard at a time." Perhaps they just didn't like the feeling that weaving the standards into their course work was a state requirement. But my questions to them were "Do you mean we should keep hidden from our candidates the state's expectation of them? Should we not let them know that what we are teaching in class will help them meet these expectations?"

I think, as well, of a day in the class I co-taught for cooperating teachers: the teachers that day emphasized the absolute reality of high-stakes assessment and the necessity of preparing students to frame their answers to questions in multiple formats, including the ones asked for in these tests. They discussed how much time they spent in teaching content and processes that they believed would help students do well on the assessments. Some even argued that the writing practice students did in preparation for the writing assessment was beneficial to students' writing. Yet, to a person, they said that their student teachers came to them understanding nothing about high-stakes assessments except that they were universally evil. Do not these cooperating teachers and their students deserve student teachers with a more nuanced view of the meaning and practice of administering the assessments? Don't teacher preparation programs have an ethical responsibility to prepare candidates for what they will experience?

Theme Two: Making Ethical Decisions

Several chapters discuss ethical decision making. For example, Tang (Chapter 4) discusses the decisions that are necessary when dealing with teacher candidates with challenges, Phillips (Chapter 5) discusses how the teacher candidates themselves need to be taught to make ethical decisions when dealing with their students, and Goble (Chapter 10) discusses ethical decision making within the context of conducting action research. In my position as a director of the office for teacher certification, I make decisions that deeply affect teacher candidates, and I don't take these lightly. It helps, however, to have a written process in place and to have help in making the decisions. Our institution has an action plan policy for teacher candidates who need extra support—ensuring that these students won't fail if we can help it. If we have to make the difficult decision of slowing a students' progress or dropping a student from a program, it is not without providing that support, and it is a joint effort of the program the candidate is in and an ad hoc committee that has the students' due process in mind. Still, there are always gray areas, and the chapters in this volume clearly acknowledge the need to reference ethical standards.

Theme Three: Honoring Student Voices

Oldfather (1995) discusses the power of honoring student voices, and her views on this strike me as being a strong theme of this volume—another foundation of ethical educational behavior. Dowdy (Chapter 3), Phillips (Chapter 5), Lassonde (Chapter 8) and Cartwright (Chapter 13), for example, all discuss the necessity of truly listening to students: Dowdy, when she listened to the subtext evident in her Harlem students' misbehavior; Phillips in honoring the confidentiality of the students with whom she worked; Lassonde in her attempts to be truly a part of each one of her students' lives and becoming, at times, their advocate to other adults; and Cartwright in relinquishing her own research agenda to honor a student's wish not to participate. But Murphy and Alexander (Chapter 2) trouble this notion by bringing up the ethical dilemma involved in valuing students' meanings while at the same time persuading them to change their beliefs and ideas. Pintrich, Marx, and Boyle (1993) note the paradoxical relationship between a student's existing knowledge and change. True learning requires a connection between what one already knows and the new information. In many cases, the student can neatly assimilate a new idea into an existing network of ideas. But when a teacher desires to *change* a student's existing idea, the relationship between the new idea and the old one is negative. The old belief has to be discarded for the new belief to take hold.

How does a teacher honor a student's belief while undermining it? When is it right to do that? I recall a time when I was working in an honors high school physics class. I had just finished demonstrating and explaining to a student that gravity affected all objects in the same way regardless of weight. Having had a non-scientific conception about gravity, he became angry and told me he couldn't believe I had just *told* him that. I obviously had not honored his existing belief—and the fact that he had an image of his career as an engineer, his father was an engineer, and he was an "A" student who was supposed to know better. His belief did change—he talked to his physics teacher after class, talked to his dad, did extra readings, and "got over it." However, I also learned yet another lesson.

In an earlier publication, I wrote several scenarios about persuasive teaching (Hynd, 2001). In one scenario, Mrs. Jones is a literature aficionado who is constantly urging her students to read literature outside of the school day. In another, Mrs. Burton has students read and discuss a persuasive text arguing against alcohol consumption. In a third, Mr. Dahl teaches a distinctly military perspective of history, and in a fourth, Mrs. Fong teaches her physics students that their intuitive beliefs about gravity are non-scientific and, thus, wrong. In each of these scenarios, the teacher has a particular perspective that he or she feels it is his or her *ethical responsibility* to impose on students. When is this imposition called for?

My take on this is that we cannot make these decisions without taking into account the larger context—we cannot make these decisions alone, with the door to the classroom closed and without the backing of the school and larger community. Lassonde discusses positioning (the necessity of placing yourself within the context), and this theory seems relevant in helping us determine what we can and cannot persuade students to believe. We are, indeed, responsible to the contexts in which we find ourselves. In the case of the scenarios mentioned above, few would argue against changing students' beliefs about gravity to more scientific ones, but teaching only a military perspective on history ignores the national history standards and, one would hope, the state and local history curriculum goals. If Mrs. Jones insists that students read literature outside of the school, she is ignoring their right to read (or not) the kinds of materials they and their families wish them to read—what the French novelist Pennac (2006) describes as the tendency of teachers to "torture" kids with books.

At the same time we must operate within community contexts; however, we bear the immense responsibility of voicing our valid ethical concerns. Dyer (Chapter 11) argues that speaking with an "audacious voice" is empowering. In instances where students are truly endangered, it is also ethical. That is, we shouldn't remain silent in the face of injustice just because the community in which we operate tolerates it. Holocaust survivors are keenly aware of the price of silence. Therein lies the delicate balance. How do we know when to listen, when to remain silent, and when to speak? How do we know which perspectives to embrace and which ones to discount? How do we help our students become open to different perspectives without being swayed by those that are unethical? We will come back to those questions later. My husband, Tim Shanahan, recently wrote,

> The power of prior knowledge—what we already know and believe when we begin to read something—can overwhelm an author's message. We spend much time these days directing kids to use their prior knowledge in reading comprehension lessons, but we should devote at least as much effort to showing them how to read against what they already think they know. (2007, p. 18)

I would add that we should also devote at least as much effort to showing them how to evaluate the validity of an author's message. In fact, we should not just teach it, but model the process in our daily lives in classrooms.

Theme Four: Honoring Our Colleagues' Voices

We have an ethical obligation to listen to our colleagues in the same way we listen to our students. This obligation was another theme in this book. Researchers who use particular research paradigms sometimes position that use in a moral framework. Some experimental researchers may believe, for instance, that in distancing themselves from their participants and in relying on objective evaluation, they mitigate the tendency to let their prior beliefs color what they observe; thus, their research is more ethical. Some qualitative researchers, on the other hand, may believe that in immersing themselves as participants in the research setting, they are better able to observe the full range of human behavior relating to the questions they are answering; thus, their research is more ethical. In reality, there are ethical concerns with any kind of research, as deftly pointed out by several authors of this volume. Smith (Chapter 7) discusses the rationale for federal and local regulations of human research, Cartwright (Chapter 13) discusses the importance of ensuring that students do not suffer because of their participation in research studies, and Shaumbaugh (Chapter 14) discusses the need for openness, honesty, and reflection in studying oneself. In relation to quantitative research, for example, Cartwright discusses the dilemma posed by a successful intervention. In such a case, the control group receives a less successful treatment, and, thus, it is relatively disadvantaged compared with the group receiving the intervention. Is this ethical? She argues that the control group needs to receive the intervention too after data collection is complete. Regarding qualitative research, what obligation does the researcher have to engage in member checking and triangulation? What obligation does the researcher have to maintain confidentiality in the face of observations of misconduct? What obligation does the researcher have to remain true to the perspectives of those who are being observed rather than to her own biases?

But it is not just that both qualitative and quantitative research paradigms have ethical concerns, it is the blindness with which researchers who align themselves in camps view the other side that has me concerned. Essentially, we are back to considering the same issues raised in theme three. How do we listen to others, (in this case our colleagues') perspectives, remain open to new ideas, and know when it is right to change our existing beliefs in the face of the new data.

Chinn and Brewer (1992) discuss the ways in which individuals react when confronted with anomalous data. They say that individuals have to resolve three basic problems: (1) they have to decide whether they believe the data; (2) they have to decide whether the anomalous data can be explained and, if so, how the data are to be explained; and (3) they have to decide whether the data require a change in their current theory.

Chinn and Brewer then postulate seven ways to solve those three problems: (1) *ignore* the data and retain their existing belief; (2) *reject* the data and retain their existing belief; (3) *exclude* the data from the domain of their belief; (4) hold the data in *abeyance* and retain their belief; (5) *reinterpret* the data and retain their belief; (6) reinterpret the data and make *peripheral changes* to their belief; and (7) *change* their belief, possibly in favor of the anomalous data.

Note that in only one of the cases is the outcome a substantive change in belief. There are many more ways to retain an existing belief than there are to change it. What does this fact have to do with ethical behavior? I believe I have an ethical obligation to take new information into account—not to automatically reject it, exclude it, reinterpret it, or put it aside. Others hold this view as well—Hirsch (1967) argues that even though we may never be able truly to understand a written message exactly as it was intended, we still have a moral obligation to try. My husband, Tim, in discussing this notion, writes, "As soon as I can determine that what you have written is absurd, profound, or beautiful, there is an even greater responsibility for me to get it right" (Shanahan, 2007, p. 18. Getting it right means not overstating, understating, or otherwise misrepresenting the idea to oneself or others.

Getting the message right is part of the ethical task. Determining its credibility is another part. If we want to engage in ethical behavior, we have to be able to determine whether our own views are valid and be willing to change our minds in the face of views that are more valid than our own. Furthermore, we have to teach our students to do the same. But how do we determine credibility?

The real challenge is not only to engage in this type of ethical analysis of our colleagues' differing perspectives but also to engage in meaningful and respectful communication regarding them. The faculty at my institution are struggling to do this, with the "social justice" faculty engaged in heartfelt and difficult conversations with other faculty who believe they have similar goals but feel their more conventional discourse is silenced. I believe we have an ethical obligation to have this conversation—to figure out how to talk to one another with respect and courage and to not overstep the bounds of propriety.

Synthesis of Ethical Lessons Learned

In this chapter, I have discussed the themes I was drawn to as I read the other chapters in this book: teaching what needs to be taught, making ethical decisions, and honoring students and each other's opinions. Within these themes, however, I'm struck by a kind of "pay it forward" idea. That is, if a teacher educator treats his colleagues with respect, listens to and remains open to their ideas (tries to "get it right," doesn't misrepresent either his own or another's view), and then makes informed decisions about what to believe and how to act on the basis of some well-thought-out criteria, this teacher educator becomes a model for his teacher candidate. And the teacher candidate, if influenced to engage in the same behavior, becomes a model for his student, and so on.

If we learned how to do that, how to be aware that our opinions are just opinions and to honor a person's beliefs even though we may not change our minds because of them, perhaps education wouldn't be in the mess it is in today. We wouldn't have gone through the "Reading Wars," there wouldn't be calls for a federal criminal investigation regarding the way NCLB has been implemented, and our students would be equipped with strategies for engaging in ethical teaching and learning.

Questions for Consideration

Think of a time when you changed your mind about something you previously believed in. What caused the change?

Choose an issue about which you have strong beliefs. How do these beliefs affect your teaching and learning?

Imagine that you would like your students to adopt your belief. What ethical considerations would you need to think about as you planned a lesson? How would this lesson proceed?

References

Chinn, C. A., & Brewer, W. F. (1992). Psychological responses to anomalous data. *Proceedings of the Fourteenth Annual Conference of the Cognitive Science Society* (pp. 165–170). Hillsdale, NJ: Lawrence Erlbaum.

Hirsch, E. D. (1967). *Validity in interpretation.* New Haven: Yale University Press.

Hynd, C. (2001). Teaching as persuasion. *Theory into Practice, 40*(4), 270–277.

Oldfather, P. (1995). Songs "come back to them": Students experiences as researchers. *Theory into Practice, 34*(2), 131–137.

Pennac, D. (2006). *The rights of the reader.* London: Walker Books.

Pintrich, P. R., Marx, R. W., & Boyle, R. A. (1993). Beyond cold conceptual change: The role of motivational beliefs and classroom contextual factors in the process of conceptual change. *Review of Educational Research, 63*(2), 167–199.

Shanahan, T. (2007). Lessons in the ethics of literacy. *Reading Today, 24*(5), 18.

Contributors

Patricia A. Alexander, Ph.D., is professor and distinguished scholar teacher in the Department of Human Development, University of Maryland, College Park. She teaches graduate and undergraduate courses in cognition and learning and educational psychology. Her research focuses on students' growing competence in reading and other academic domains and the interactions among knowledge, strategies, and interest in those domains. Before receiving her doctorate in 1981, Dr. Alexander was a middle school teacher and a reading specialist.

Allen Berger is Heckert professor emeritus, Miami University, Oxford, Ohio. He taught high school for five years in Utica and Rochester, New York, and has been a tenured faculty member at Southern Illinois University, the University of Alberta, the University of Pittsburgh, and Miami University. He has written approximately four hundred articles on education. He lives in Savannah, Georgia. The essay he refers to in his foreword, "Questions of Ethics," was the basis of a speech he gave at the World Congress on Reading in Hamburg, Germany.

Kelly B. Cartwright, Ph.D., is currently an associate professor of psychology at Christopher Newport University (CNU) in Newport News, Virginia, where she teaches undergraduate courses in child development, cognitive development, and research methods. Cartwright also serves on the steering committee for the interdisciplinary Teacher Preparation Program at CNU, for which she teaches graduate courses in reading. Her research focuses on the roles of cognitive development and cognitive flexibility in literacy processes, family and gender influences on literacy development, and preservice reading teacher education.

Joanne Kilgour Dowdy, Ph.D., is an associate professor of adolescent/adult literacy in the Department of Teaching, Leadership, and Curriculum and Instruction at the College of Education, Kent State University, Kent, Ohio. Her major research interests include women and literacy, drama in education, and video technology in qualitative research instruction. Her fifth book is about black women in higher education.

Debra Dyer, Ed.D., has spent thirty-two years in an upstate New York public school district teaching ten years in the fifth and sixth grades and the last twenty-two years in kindergarten. She received her doctoral degree from Binghamton University (SUNY). Currently, she is an assistant professor at Keuka College in both the early childhood and master's degree programs. Dr. Dyer's research and writing pursuits are in the areas of play-based curriculum, early childhood advocacy, and passion in teaching.

Deborah Eldridge, Ph.D., is a professor and chair of the Department of Curriculum and Teaching in the College of Education and Human Services at Montclair State University. Although she specializes in literacy, Dr. Eldridge writes, presents, and researches in the areas of teacher preparation for reading instruction, the arts in education, and technology integration in teacher education.

Gina A. Goble, Ed.S., has been a classroom teacher for seventeen years, specializing in the urban, bilingual, at-risk population. For the past three years she has been on the editorial board of *The Reading Teacher*, a journal of the International Reading Association. She earned her M.Ed. in Urban Education from New Jersey City University and an Ed.S. from Rutgers University in Literacy Education. She spent a period of her teaching career working in a model program sponsored by the New Jersey Education Association, one aspect of which was job-embedded professional development.

Jennifer Goeke, Ph.D., is an assistant professor of special education in the Department of Curriculum and Teaching in the College of Education and Human Services at Montclair State University. Dr. Goeke writes, presents, and researches in the areas of preservice teachers' experiences with inclusion, peer mentoring, and case methodology in special education teacher education. She also presents and consults on research-based instructional strategies for inclusion, co-teaching, and differentiated instruction.

Susan E. Israel, Ph.D., researches in the area of reading comprehension and child-mind development as it relates to literacy processes in reading and writing. She has worked with the Alliance for Catholic Education at the University of Notre Dame. She was awarded the 2005 Panhellenic Council Outstanding

Professor Award at the University of Dayton. She was the 1998 recipient of the teacher researcher grant from the International Reading Association, of which she has been a member for over a decade. She enjoys reading nonfiction books, gardening, and quilting. Her favorite novelist is Matthew Pearl, who writes historical mysteries.

Cynthia A. Lassonde, Ph.D., is assistant professor of elementary education and reading and teaches undergraduate and graduate literacy courses at the State University of New York College at Oneonta. A former elementary teacher and teacher researcher for more years than she'd like to admit, she now lists among her research interests the teaching of writing and critical inquiry pedagogy. She has authored numerous articles in professional education journals such as *Language Arts, Literacy Teaching and Learning, Support for Learning,* and *Youth and Society,* many of which are products of teacher research in her elementary and college classrooms. The two professional responsibilities she enjoys most are her positions as editor of the New York Association of Colleges for Teacher Education's journal *Excelsior: Leadership in Teaching and Learning* and chair of the Teacher as Researcher Subcommittee of the International Reading Association. But her life's joys are her daughters Ann, Jill, and Kelly and her husband Mark.

Daqi Li, Ed.D., is assistant professor in the Educational Psychology and Counseling Department at the State University of New York, Oneonta. Dr. Daqi Li teaches undergraduate and graduate courses in special education. His current research interests include learning disabilities and technology applications.

P. Karen Murphy, Ph.D., is an associate professor of educational psychology at Penn State University. She teaches graduate and undergraduate courses in knowledge and beliefs, learning theory, and educational statistics. Her master's research was in the area of ethics, and her current research projects pertain to the impact of students' and teachers' knowledge, beliefs, and interest on learning, the influence of technology in text-based comprehension, and the role of group discussion in reading comprehension.

Nithya Narayanaswamy Iyer, Ed.D., is an assistant professor in the Department of Educational Psychology and Counseling at the State University of New York College at Oneonta, where she teaches courses in the psychological foundations of education. Her current research interests include teacher induction and multiple intelligences.

Emily Phillips, Ph.D., NCC, is a former school counselor and mental health clinician. She currently is a counselor educator, training school counselors at the State University of New York at Oneonta.

Linda Pratt, Ed.D., is the executive director of teacher education and professor of education at Elmira College in New York. She has taught graduate and undergraduate literacy courses and has worked with preservice teachers in the Bahamas and the United States. Dr. Pratt's scholarly achievements include co-authoring textbooks on pre-school and kindergarten literacy and on transcultural children's literature. Moreover, she has given presentations on literacy and preservice teacher education in Asia, the Bahamas, the Caribbean, Canada, Eastern and Western Europe, South America, and the United States.

Neal Shambaugh, Ph.D., is an associate professor of instructional design and technology and the IDT program coordinator in the College of Human Resources and Education at West Virginia University. His research interests include instructional design, teacher education action research and technology use, novice problem solving, and visual literacy.

Cynthia Shanahan, Ph.D., is a professor in the University of Illinois at Chicago (UIC) Department of Curriculum and Instruction and executive director of the Council on Teacher Education (CTE). As the director of the CTE, Dr. Shanahan coordinates the activities of the various educational certification programs across five colleges at UIC. As a professor in the Department of Curriculum and Instruction, she teaches in the programs of literacy, language and culture, and secondary education. Her research interests include learning from text, and she is currently engaged in a project that focuses on reading in the disciplines of history, chemistry, and mathematics.

Joye Smith, Ed.D., is an assistant professor of TESOL in the Department of Middle and High School at Lehman College, the City University of New York, where she teaches second-language acquisition, methods of teaching English grammar, and research methods. She coordinates the M.S.Ed. TESOL program and serves on the institutional review board of her college. Her current interests include alternative assessment, sector analysis, and collaboration between mainstream and ESOL teachers.

Katherine A. Dougherty Stahl, Ed.D., is an assistant professor in the literacy division of Steinhardt School of Education's Teaching and Learning Department at New York University. She taught in public elementary school classrooms for more than twenty-five years. Her research interests focus on reading acquisition, including the reading fluency and reading comprehension of novice readers.

Ying Tang, Ph.D., NCC, is assistant professor at the State University of New York at Oneonta and a counselor educator. Her research interests include counselor supervision, career counseling, and instructional technology.

Kenneth J. Weiss, Ed.D., is currently an associate professor in the Department of Reading and Language Arts at Elmira College in New York, where he teaches both undergraduate and graduate courses in developmental reading. Ken has taught in higher education for more than fifteen years and was formerly an elementary school teacher and, with his wife, owner of a children's bookstore. Ken's research focus is on reader response, how the use of text messaging affects college students' literacy and social skills, and issues of global literacy.